Q: Skills for Success

INTRO

LISTENING AND SPEAKING

Teacher's Handbook

Kristin D. Sherman

OXFORD
UNIVERSITY PRESS

OXFORD
UNIVERSITY PRESS

198 Madison Avenue
New York, NY 10016 USA

Great Clarendon Street, Oxford, OX2 6DP, United Kingdom

Oxford University Press is a department of the University of Oxford.
It furthers the University's objective of excellence in research, scholarship,
and education by publishing worldwide. Oxford is a registered trade
mark of Oxford University Press in the UK and in certain other countries

© Oxford University Press 2011

The moral rights of the author have been asserted.

First published in 2011
2015 2014 2013 2012 2011
10 9 8 7 6 5 4 3 2 1

Photocopying

General Manager, American ELT: Laura Pearson
Publisher: Stephanie Karras
Associate Publishing Manager: Sharon Sargent
Associate Development Editor: Rebecca Mostov
Director, ADP: Susan Sanguily
Executive Design Manager: Maj-Britt Hagsted
Associate Design Manager: Michael Steinhofer
Electronic Production Manager: Julie Armstrong
Production Artist: Elissa Santos
Cover Design: Michael Steinhofer
Production Coordinator: Elizabeth Matsumoto

ISBN: 978-0-19-475647-1 Listening and Speaking Intro Teacher's
Handbook Pack
ISBN: 978-0-19-475663-1 Listening and Speaking Intro Teacher's Handbook
ISBN: 978-0-19-475666-2 Listening and Speaking Intro/Reading and Writing
Intro Testing Program CD-ROM
ISBN: 978-0-19-475643-3 Q Online Practice Teacher Access Code Card

Printed in China

This book is printed on paper from certified and well-managed sources.

ACKNOWLEDGEMENTS
The publishers would like to thank the following for their kind permission
reproduce photographs:
p. iv Marcin Krygier/iStockphoto; xiii Rüstem GÜRLER/iStockphoto

CONTENTS

WELCOME TO Q:Skills for Success

Q: Skills for Success is a six-level series with two strands, *Reading and Writing* and *Listening and Speaking*.

READING AND WRITING

LISTENING AND SPEAKING

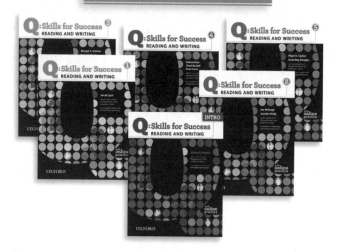

WITH Q ONLINE PRACTICE web+

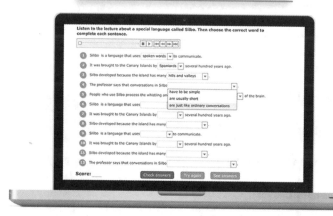

STUDENT AND TEACHER INFORMED

Q: Skills for Success is the result of an extensive development process involving thousands of teachers and hundreds of students around the world. Their views and opinions helped shape the content of the series. *Q* is grounded in teaching theory as well as real-world classroom practice, making it the most learner-centered series available.

Highlights of the *Q: Skills for Success* Teacher's Handbook

LEARNING OUTCOMES

As you probably know from your own teaching experience, students want to know the point of a lesson. They want to know the "why" even when they understand the "how." In the classroom, the "why" is the learning outcome, and to be successful, students need to know it. The learning outcome provides a clear reason for classroom work and helps students meaningfully access new material.

Each unit in Oxford's *Q: Skills for Success* series builds around a thought-provoking question related to that unit's unique learning outcome. Students learn vocabulary to answer the unit question; consider new information related to the unit's theme that utilizes this vocabulary; use this information to think critically about new questions; and use those answers to practice the new listening, vocabulary, grammar, pronunciation, and speaking skills they need to achieve the unit's learning outcome.

Each aspect of the learning process in the Q series builds toward completing the learning outcome. This interconnected process of considering new information is at the heart of a critical thinking approach and forms the basis of the students' work in each unit of the Q series. At the end of the unit, students complete a practical project built around the learning outcome.

Learning outcomes create expectations in the classroom: expectations of what students will learn, what teachers will teach, and what lessons will focus on. Students benefit because they know they need to learn content for a purpose; teachers benefit because they can plan activities that reinforce the knowledge and skills students need to complete the learning outcome. In short, learning outcomes provide the focus that lessons need.

UNIT 6

Unit QUESTION
Who makes you laugh?

Laughter

LISTENING • listening for specific information
VOCABULARY • synonyms
GRAMMAR • simple present for informal narratives
PRONUNCIATION • simple present third-person -s/-es
SPEAKING • using eye contact, pause, and tone of voice

LEARNING OUTCOME
Use appropriate eye contact, tone of voice, and pauses to tell a funny story or a joke to your classmates.

Tell a Story or Joke	20 points	15 points	10 points	0 points
Student told the joke or funny story easily (without long pauses or reading) and was easy to understand (spoke clearly and at a good speed).				
Student used the simple present tense correctly.				
Student used vocabulary from the unit.				
Student used eye contact, pauses, and tone of voice to effectively tell the joke or funny story.				
Student correctly pronounced third person -s/-es.				

Total points: _____
Comments:

In this example unit, students are asked to think about who makes them laugh while preparing to tell their own joke or funny story.

The unit assignment ties into that unit's unique learning outcome.

Clear assessments allow both teachers and students to comment on and measure learner outcomes.

Q Unit Assignment: Tell a joke or a funny story

Unit Question (5 minutes)

Refer students back to the ideas they discussed at the beginning of the unit about who makes them laugh. Cue students if necessary by asking specific questions about the content of the unit: *Why did people think Jackie Chan was funny? What advice did we hear about how to be funny? What skills can you use to make your jokes and stories more entertaining?*

Learning Outcome

1. Tie the Unit Assignment to the unit learning outcome. Say: *The outcome for this unit is to use appropriate eye contact, tone of voice, and pauses to tell a funny story or a joke to your classmates. This Unit Assignment is going to let you show that you can do that as well as correctly use and pronounce the simple present.*

CRITICAL THINKING

A critical thinking approach asks students to process new information and to learn how to apply that information to a new situation. Teachers might set learning outcomes to give students targets to hit—for example: "After this lesson, give three reasons why people immigrate"—and the materials and exercises in the lesson provide students with the knowledge and skills to think critically and discover *their* three reasons.

Questions are important catalysts in the critical thinking process. Questions encourage students to reflect on and apply their knowledge to new situations. Students and teachers work together to understand, analyze, synthesize, and evaluate the lesson's questions and content to reach the stated outcomes. As students become more familiar with these stages of the critical thinking process, they will be able to use new information to complete tasks more efficiently and in unique and meaningful ways.

Tip) Critical Thinking

In Activity B, you have to **restate**, or say again in perhaps a different way, some of the information you learned in the two readings. **Restating** is a good way to review information.

B (10 minutes)

1. Introduce the Unit Question, *Why do people immigrate to other countries?* Ask related information questions or questions about personal experience to help students prepare for answering the more abstract unit question: *Did you immigrate to this country? What were your reasons for leaving your home country? What were your reasons for choosing your new country? What did you bring with you?*

2. Tell students: *Let's start off our discussion by listing reasons why people might immigrate. For example, we could start our list with* finding work *because many people look for jobs in new countries. But there are many other reasons why people immigrate. What else can we think of?*

Throughout the Student Book, *Critical Thinking Tips* accompany certain activities, helping students to practice and understand these critical thinking skills.

Critical Thinking Tip (1 minute)

1. Read the tip aloud.

2. Tell students that restating also helps to ensure that they have understood something correctly. After reading a new piece of information, they should try to restate it to a classmate who has also read the information, to ensure that they both have the same understanding of information.

The *Q Teacher's Handbook* features notes offering questions for expanded thought and discussion.

CRITICAL Q EXPANSION ACTIVITIES

The *Q Teacher's Handbook* expands on the critical thinking approach with the Critical Q Expansion Activities. These activities allow teachers to facilitate more practice for their students. The Critical Q Expansion Activities supplement the *Q Student Book* by expanding on skills and language students are practicing.

In today's classrooms, it's necessary that students have the ability to apply the skills they have learned to new situations with materials they have never seen before. *Q*'s focus on critical thinking and the *Q Teacher's Handbook's* emphasis on practicing critical thinking skills through the Critical Q Expansion Activities prepares students to excel in this important skill.

The easy-to-use activity suggestions increase student practice and success with critical thinking skills.

Critical Q: Expansion Activity

Outlining

1. Explain to students: *A popular way to prepare to outline one's ideas is to use a cluster map. In a cluster map, a big circle is drawn in the middle of a page or on the board, and a main point is written inside it—**this will become the topic sentence in the outline.***

2. Then explain: *Next, lines are drawn away from the circle and new, smaller circles are attached to the other end of those lines. Inside each of the smaller circles, ideas are written which relate to the main point—**these become supporting sentences in the outline.***

Both the academic and professional worlds are becoming increasingly interdependent. The toughest problems are solved only when looked at from multiple perspectives. Success in the 21st century requires more than just core academic knowledge—though that is still crucial. Now, successful students have to collaborate, innovate, adapt, be self-directed, be flexible, be creative, be tech-literate, practice teamwork, and be accountable—both individually and in groups.

Q approaches language learning in light of these important 21st Century Skills. Each unit asks students to practice many of these attributes, from collaboration to innovation to accountability, while they are learning new language and content. The *Q Student Books* focus on these increasingly important skills with unique team, pair, and individual activities. Additionally, the *Q Teacher's Handbooks* provide support with easy-to-use 21st Century Skill sections for teachers who want to incorporate skills like "openness to other people's ideas and opinions" into their classrooms but aren't sure where to start.

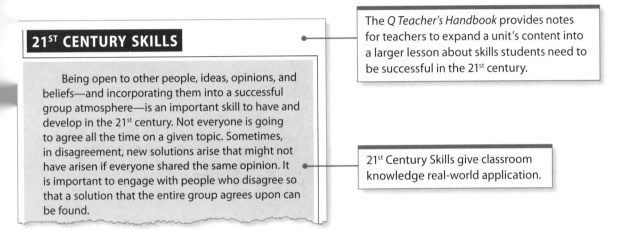

21ST CENTURY SKILLS

Being open to other people, ideas, opinions, and beliefs—and incorporating them into a successful group atmosphere—is an important skill to have and develop in the 21st century. Not everyone is going to agree all the time on a given topic. Sometimes, in disagreement, new solutions arise that might not have arisen if everyone shared the same opinion. It is important to engage with people who disagree so that a solution that the entire group agrees upon can be found.

The *Q Teacher's Handbook* provides notes for teachers to expand a unit's content into a larger lesson about skills students need to be successful in the 21st century.

21st Century Skills give classroom knowledge real-world application.

Q ONLINE PRACTICE

Q Online Practice is an online workbook that gives students quick access to all-new content in a range of additional practice activities. The interface is intuitive and user-friendly, allowing students to focus on enhancing their language skills.

For the teacher, *Q Online Practice* includes a digital grade book providing immediate and accurate assessment of each student's progress. Straightforward individual student or class reports can be viewed onscreen, printed, or exported, giving you comprehensive feedback on what students have mastered or where they need more help.

Teacher's Access Code Cards for the digital grade book are available upon adoption or for purchase. Use the access code to register for your *Q Online Practice* account at www.Qonlinepractice.com.

These features of the *Q: Skills for Success* series enable you to help your students develop the skills they need to succeed in their future academic and professional careers. By using learning outcomes, critical thinking, and 21st century skills, you help students gain a deeper knowledge of the material they are presented with, both in and out of the classroom.

Q connects critical thinking, language skills, and learning outcomes.

LANGUAGE SKILLS

Explicit skills instruction enables students to meet their academic and professional goals.

LEARNING OUTCOMES

Clearly identified **learning outcomes** focus students on the goal of their instruction.

UNIT **3**
Education

LISTENING	listening for examples
VOCABULARY	using the dictionary: antonyms
GRAMMAR	adjectives; adverbs + adjectives
PRONUNCIATION	sentence stress
SPEAKING	giving opinions

LEARNING OUTCOME
Share your opinions to plan a perfect school and present your plan to the class.

Unit QUESTION
What makes a good school?

PREVIEW THE UNIT

A Answer the questions about your school. Then compare with a partner.

1. How many students go to your school? _____

2. How many students are in your class? _____

3. What are two clubs at your school? _____
   _____

4. What are two sports teams at your school? _____
   _____

B Look at the photo. Where are the students? What are they doing?

C Discuss the Unit Question above with your classmates.

Listen to *The Q Classroom*, Track 21 on CD 1, to hear other answers.

32   UNIT 3

33

CRITICAL THINKING

Thought-provoking **unit questions** engage students with the topic and provide a **critical thinking framework** for the unit.

 Having the learning outcome is important because it gives students and teachers a clear idea of what the point of each task/activity in the unit is.
Lawrence Lawson, Palomar College, California

PREVIEW THE LISTENING

LANGUAGE SKILLS

Listening texts provide input on the unit question and give **exposure to academic content.**

Let's Take a Tour

A. You are going to listen to Sarah Carter, a student, give a tour of Watson University. Look at the map. Then match the names of the places with the definitions.

Watson University

CRITICAL THINKING

Students **discuss** their opinions of each listening text and **analyze** how it changes their perspective on the unit question.

Q WHAT DO YOU THINK?

A. Give your opinion of the following statements. Circle *Yes* or *No*.

 WATSON UNIVERSITY

What makes a good school?

1. Yes No It's important to learn a foreign language in school.
2. Yes No It's important to have good friends at school.
3. Yes No Every school needs a lot of clubs and teams.
4. Yes No A good school has computers for students to use.

 One of the best features is your focus on developing materials of a high "interest level."
Troy Hammond, Tokyo Gakugei University, International Secondary School, Japan

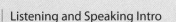

Explicit skills instruction prepares students for academic success.

LANGUAGE SKILLS

Explicit instruction and practice in listening, speaking, grammar, pronunciation, and vocabulary skills **help students achieve language proficiency.**

LEARNING OUTCOMES

Practice activities allow students to **master the skills** before they are evaluated at the end of the unit.

| Speaking Skill | Giving opinions | web |

CD 1
Track 25

Use the phrases *I think that . . .* and *In my opinion, . . .* to give an opinion.

I **think that** students need computers.
In my opinion, small classes are important.

You can answer opinions with *I agree* or *I disagree* followed by your opinion.

A: I **think that** our school is great.
B: I **agree.** I think that the classes are interesting.
C: I **disagree.** In my opinion, the classes are too big.

CD 1
Track 26

A. Listen and complete the conversations. Use expressions from the box above. Compare answers with a partner.

1. A: _____ a good school gives a lot of tests.
   Then students study every day.
   B: _____. Class discussions make students study.

2. A: _____ sports are really important. Students need healthy bodies.
   B: _____. Exercise is very important.

3. A: _____ the food in our dining commons isn't very good. I don't like it!
   B: _____, _____ it tastes terrible. I usually cook my own food.

4. A: _____ we need a new library. The building is really old.
   B: _____. I like our library. _____ it's beautiful.

Tip for Success

When you write *In my opinion,* use a comma. Don't use a comma after *I think that.*

| Pronunciation | Sentence stress | web |

When you speak, you **stress** certain **important words.** This means you say them more loudly.

- Important words—like nouns, adjectives, and adverbs—give the information in the sentences.
- You do not usually stress words like pronouns, prepositions, *a/an/the,* the verb *be,* or the verb *do.*

CD 1
Track 23

There are **two sports fields.**
The **museum** is **not interesting.**
We go to **school** in a **really dangerous neighborhood.**
Do you **have** a **class today?**

CD 1
Track 24

A. Underline the stressed words. Listen and check your answers. Then practice the sentences with a partner.

1. Does the school have a lacrosse team?
2. I have two classes in the morning.
3. We want a safe and clean school.
4. The college is in a dangerous city.
5. The coffee shops have free Internet access.
6. What is a good school?
7. Our sports field is pretty big.
8. My school is really great!
9. The buses to his school are very slow.
10. When does the class begin?

lacrosse team

B. In your notebook, write five sentences about your school. Use adjectives and the adverbs *pretty, really, very,* and *extremely.*

C. Trade papers with a partner. Underline the stressed words. Then practice the sentences.

The campus is extremely large.

The tasks are simple, accessible, user-friendly, and very useful.
Jessica March, American University of Sharjah, U.A.E.

Q Online Practice provides all new content for additional practice in an easy-to-use online workbook. Every student book includes a *Q Online Practice access code card*. Use the access code to register for your *Q Online Practice* account at www.Qonlinepractice.com.

Building Vocabulary   Using the dictionary

Tip for Success

Learning antonyms is a good way to build your vocabulary quickly. When you learn a new adjective, try to find out what its antonym is. Learners' dictionaries often give useful synonyms and antonyms.

Antonyms are words with opposite meanings. For example, *good* and *bad* are antonyms. Most forms of words—nouns, verbs, adjectives, adverbs, and prepositions—can have antonyms.

The dictionary often gives antonyms in the definition of a word. In the example below, notice the antonym of *hard*.

> **hard**¹ 🗝 /hard/ *adjective* (hard·er, hard·est)
> **1** not soft: *These apples are very hard.* • *I couldn't sleep because the bed was too hard.* ⊃ **ANTONYM soft**
> **2** difficult to do or understand: *The exam was very hard.* • *hard work* ⊃ **ANTONYM easy**
> **3** full of problems: *He's had **a hard life.*** ⊃ **ANTONYM easy**
> **4** not kind or gentle: *She is very **hard on** her children.* ⊃ **ANTONYM soft**

All dictionary entries are taken from the *Oxford Basic American Dictionary for learners of English* © Oxford University Press 2011.

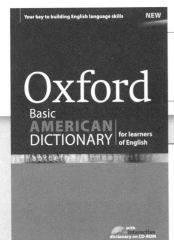

All dictionary entries are taken from the *Oxford Basic American Dictionary for learners of English.*

A **research-based vocabulary program** focuses students on the words they need to know academically and professionally, using skill strategies based on the same research as the Oxford dictionaries.

The ***Oxford Basic American Dictionary for learners of English*** was designed with English learners in mind, and provides extra learning tools for pronunciation, verb types, basic grammar structures, and more.

The Oxford 2000 Keywords 🗝

The Oxford 2000 keywords encompasses **the 2000 most important words to learn in English**. It is based on a comprehensive analysis of the Oxford English Corpus, a two-billion-word collection of English text, and on extensive research with both language and pedagogical experts.

The Academic Word List **AWL**

The Academic Word List was created by Averil Coxhead and contains **570 words that are commonly used in academic English**, such as in textbooks or articles across a wide range of academic subject areas. These words are a great place to start if you are studying English for academic purposes.

Clear learning outcomes focus students on the goals of instruction.

LEARNING OUTCOMES

A culminating unit assignment evaluates the students' **mastery of the learning outcome.**

| Unit Assignment | Plan a perfect school |

 In this assignment, you plan a perfect school and present your plan to your class. This can be a high school, university, or other kind of school. As you prepare, think about the Unit Question, "What makes a good school?" and use the Self-Assessment checklist on page 44.

CONSIDER THE IDEAS

 CD 1 Track 27

Listen to a group present their ideas for a perfect school. Check (✓) the ideas that they give. Then compare answers with a partner.

☐ 1. The perfect school is large.
☐ 2. The classes are very small.
☐ 3. The school has a lot of clubs, like a movie club and a soccer club.
☐ 4. There is a big gym.
☐ 5. Students get free computers.
☐ 6. The school is in a big city.
☐ 7. Apartments in town are cheap and beautiful.
☐ 8. Food on campus is cheap.

LEARNER CENTERED

Track Your Success allows students to **assess their own progress** and provides guidance on remediation.

Check (✓) the skills you learned. If you need more work on a skill, refer to the page(s) in parentheses.

LISTENING	I can listen for examples. (p. 36)
VOCABULARY	I can use the dictionary to understand antonyms. (p. 37)
GRAMMAR	I can use adjectives and adverbs + adjectives. (p. 39)
PRONUNCIATION	I can use correct sentence stress. (p. 41)
SPEAKING	I can give my opinion. (p. 42)
LEARNING OUTCOME	I can share my opinions to plan a perfect school and present the plan to the class. (p. 43)

 Students can check their learning … and they can focus on the essential points when they study.

Suh Yoomi, Seoul, South Korea

For the student

- **Easy-to-use:** a simple interface allows students to focus on enhancing their speaking and listening skills, not learning a new software program
- **Flexible:** for use anywhere there's an Internet connection
- **Access code card:** a *Q Online Practice* access code is included with this book—use the access code to register for *Q Online Practice* at www.Qonlinepractice.com

For the teacher

- **Simple yet powerful:** automatically grades student exercises and tracks progress
- **Straightforward:** online management system to review, print, or export reports
- **Flexible:** for use in the classroom or easily assigned as homework
- **Access code card:** with the *Q Teacher's Handbook* or sold separately

Teacher Resources

Q Teacher's Handbook gives strategic support through:

- specific teaching notes for each activity
- ideas for ensuring student participation
- multilevel strategies and expansion activities
- the answer key
- special sections on 21st century skills and critical thinking
- a *Testing Program CD-ROM* with a customizable test for each unit
- a *Q Online Practice* teacher's access code card

For additional resources visit the
Q: Skills for Success companion website at
www.oup.com/elt/teacher/Qskillsforsuccess

Q Class Audio includes:

- listening texts
- skills presentations and exercises
- *The Q Classroom*

 It's an interesting, engaging series which provides plenty of materials that are easy to use in class, as well as instructionally promising.
Donald Weasenforth, Collin College, Texas

UNIT	LISTENING	SPEAKING	VOCABULAR
1 **People** **Q** **What are you interested in?** LISTENING: Are You Interested in Art? Conversations (Greetings and Introductions)	• Identify information in an introduction • Predict content • Listen for main ideas • Listen for details	• Keep a conversation going by adding information • Keep a conversation going by showing you are thinking • Survey classmates about interests • Take notes to prepare for a presentation or discussion • Introduce a classmate	• Use collocations for hobbies and interest • Match definitions • Define new terms • Learn selected vocabulary words from the Oxford 200 keywords and the Academic Word List
2 **Friendship** **Q** **How do you make friends?** LISTENING: Making Friends A Radio Program (Social Psychology)	• Listen for examples • Predict content • Listen for main ideas • Listen for details	• Ask and answer questions • Take notes to prepare for a presentation or discussion • Give a presentation on ways to make friends • Add more information to a presentation	• Use word categories to expand vocabulary • Match definitions • Define new terms • Learn selected vocabulary words from the Oxford 2000 keywords and the Academic Word List
3 **Education** **Q** **What makes a good school?** LISTENING: Let's Take a Tour A Campus Tour (Education)	• Predict content • Listen for main ideas • Listen for details • Listen for examples	• Give opinions • Express agreement and disagreement • Support ideas with examples and details • Take notes to prepare for a presentation or discussion • Present ideas to the class	• Use the dictionary to find antonyms and expand vocabulary • Match definitions • Define new terms • Learn selected vocabulary words from the Oxford 2000 keywords and the Academic Word List
4 **Food** **Q** **How do you choose your food?** LISTENING: Lifestyles and Food Choices A Radio Interview (Food and Nutrition)	• Listen for reasons • Predict content • Listen for main ideas • Listen for details	• Take notes to prepare for a presentation or discussion • Interview a classmate about food choices • Give opinions • Discuss results with the class	• Use prefixes and suffixes • Match definitions • Define new terms • Learn selected vocabulary words from the Oxford 2000 keywords and the Academic Word List

GRAMMAR	PRONUNCIATION	CRITICAL THINKING	UNIT OUTCOME
Present of *be*; Simple present affirmative statements	• Simple present third-person *-s/-es*	• Identify sounds to demonstrate knowledge • Apply knowledge to complete a new task • Reflect on the unit question • Connect ideas and integrate information from multiple sources • Express ideas/reactions/opinions orally • Apply unit tips and use *Q Online Practice* to become a strategic learner	• Interview a classmate about his or her interests and introduce him or her to the class.
• Simple present	• Sentence intonation	• Define terms to demonstrate knowledge • Classify information to understand how things are similar and different • Apply knowledge to complete a new task • Reflect on the unit question • Connect ideas and integrate information from multiple sources • Express ideas/reactions/opinions orally • Apply unit tips and use *Q Online Practice* to become a strategic learner	• Give a presentation that describes some good ways to make friends, including details and examples.
• Adjectives; Adverbs + adjectives	• Sentence stress	• Discuss ideas to show understanding • Apply knowledge to complete a new task • Reflect on the unit question • Connect ideas and integrate information from multiple sources • Express ideas/reactions/opinions orally • Apply unit tips and use *Q Online Practice* to become a strategic learner	• Share your opinions to plan a perfect school and present your plan to the class.
• Verbs + gerunds and infinitives	• Stressed syllables	• Summarize information • Relate information to own experience • Reflect on the unit question • Connect ideas/integrate information from multiple sources • Express ideas/reactions/opinions orally • Apply unit tips and use *Q Online Practice* to become a strategic learner	• Design a survey about food and interview a classmate about his or her food choices.

UNIT	LISTENING	SPEAKING	VOCABULARY
5 Fun **Q** **What makes something fun?** LISTENING: Why Do You Come to the Park? A Report (Travel)	• Predict content • Listen for main ideas • Listen for details • Listen for reasons	• Agree with positive and negative opinions • Disagree politely • Discuss fun activities • Take notes to prepare for a presentation or discussion • Participate in a group discussion	• Use collocations with *do*, *play*, and *go* • Match definitions • Define new terms • Learn selected vocabulary words from the Oxford 200 keywords and the Academic Word List
6 Home **Q** **What makes a good home?** LISTENING 1: How Do You Like Your Home? An Informal Survey (Sociology) LISTENING 2: Housing Problems, Housing Solutions A City Meeting (Urban Planning)	• Listen for opinions • Predict content • Listen for main ideas • Listen for details	• Discuss ideas • Take notes to prepare for a presentation or discussion • Agree and disagree • Give a presentation	• Use compound nouns • Match definitions • Define new terms • Learn selected vocabulary words from the Oxford 2000 keywords and the Academic Word List
7 Weather **Q** **How does the weather affect you?** LISTENING 1: The World of Weather A Weather Report (News and Weather) LISTENING 2: Weather and Our Moods A Lecture (Psychology)	• Predict content • Listen for main ideas • Listen for details • Listen for opinions	• Ask for repetition • Ask and answer questions • Take notes to prepare for a presentation or discussion • Participate in a group discussion	• Use nouns and adjectives for weather • Match definitions • Define new terms • Learn selected vocabulary words from the Oxford 2000 keywords and the Academic Word List
8 Health **Q** **What do you do to stay healthy?** LISTENING 1: Health Watch A Podcast Interview (Health and Wellness) LISTENING 2: How Often Do You Work Out? An Interview (Behavior and Health)	• Listen for frequency • Predict content • Listen for main ideas • Listen for details	• Describe problems • Give advice • Take notes to prepare for a presentation or discussion • Conduct a survey • Ask for repetition • Discuss results	• Use adjectives ending in -ed • Match definitions • Define new terms • Learn selected vocabulary words from the Oxford 2000 keywords and the Academic Word List

GRAMMAR	PRONUNCIATION	CRITICAL THINKING	UNIT OUTCOME
• ubject and object ronouns	• Reduced pronouns	• Practice to apply information to new situations • Support ideas with reasons • Reflect on the unit question • Connect ideas/integrate information from multiple sources • Express ideas/reactions/ opinions orally • Apply unit tips and use *Q Online Practice* to become a strategic learner	• Participate in a group discussion about fun places in your area.
Prepositions of location	• Stress in compound nouns	• Identify pros and cons • Rank items and make evaluations • Apply knowledge to complete a new task • Reflect on the unit question • Connect ideas/integrate information from multiple sources • Express ideas/reactions/ opinions orally • Apply unit tips and use *Q Online Practice* to become a strategic learner	• Design your perfect home and present your design to the class.
• Adverbs of frequency	• Stressing important words	• Use a chart to organize information • Apply information to personal experience • Reflect on the unit question • Connect ideas/integrate information from multiple sources • Express ideas/reactions/ opinions orally • Apply unit tips and use *Q Online Practice* to become a strategic learner	• Participate in a group discussion about weather.
• Modals *can* and *should*	• *can, can't, should, and shouldn't*	• Relate ideas to own experience • Compare and contrast habits to understand ideas more deeply • Reflect on the unit question • Connect ideas/integrate information from multiple sources • Express ideas/reactions/ opinions orally • Apply unit tips and use *Q Online Practice* to become a strategic learner	• Create, conduct, and discuss a health survey.

UNIT	LISTENING	SPEAKING	VOCABULAR
9 Cities **What makes a city special?** **LISTENING 1:** Travel Talk A Radio Program (Geography and Travel) **LISTENING 2:** Making Positive Changes A Speech (Government and Economics)	• Predict content • Listen for main ideas • Listen for details • Listen for frequency	• Use open questions • Participate in a discussion • Take notes to prepare for a presentation or discussion • Give a presentation	• Use the dictionary to understand word families and expand vocabulary • Match definitions • Define new terms • Learn selected vocabulary words from the Oxford 200● keywords and the Academic Word List
10 Milestones **What are the most important events in someone's life?** **LISTENING 1:** Ania Filochowska: A Young Genius A Radio Quiz (Biography) **LISTENING 2:** Naguib Mahfouz: A Successful Writer A Class Presentation (Literature)	• Listen for sequence • Listen for numbers • Predict content • Listen for main ideas • Listen for details	• Take notes to prepare for a presentation or discussion • Interview a classmate • Use open questions • Give a presentation to the class	• Use phrases with *get* • Match definitions • Define new terms • Learn selected vocabulary words from the Oxford 2000 keywords and the Academic Word List

GRAMMAR	PRONUNCIATION	CRITICAL THINKING	UNIT OUTCOME
ast of *be*; Simple past ffirmative statements	• *-ed* endings	• Combine information from different sources to come up with new ideas • Discuss problems and solutions • Reflect on the unit question • Connect ideas/integrate information from multiple sources • Express ideas/reactions/ opinions orally • Apply unit tips and use *Q Online Practice* to become a strategic learner	• Give a presentation about a special city using the simple present and simple past.
Simple past with regular and irregular verbs	• Numbers with *-teen* and *-ty*	• Choose most important milestones • Apply knowledge to complete a new task • Reflect on the unit question • Connect ideas/integrate information from multiple sources • Express ideas/reactions/ opinions orally • Apply unit tips and use *Q Online Practice* to become a strategic learner	• Interview a classmate about the most important events in his or her life and present them to the class.

Unit QUESTION

What are you interested in?

People

VOCABULARY • collocations for hobbies and interests
GRAMMAR • present of *be*; simple present affirmative statements
PRONUNCIATION • simple present third-person *-s/-es*
SPEAKING • keeping a conversation going

LEARNING OUTCOME

Interview a classmate about his or her interests and introduce him or her to the class.

▶ *Listening and Speaking Intro, page 2*

Preview the Unit

Learning Outcome

1. Ask for a volunteer to read the unit skills and then the unit Learning Outcome.

2. Explain: *Your goal for the unit is to be able to interview a classmate about his or her interests and introduce him or her to the class. I will use this Learning Outcome to grade your work at the end of the unit. Focus on learning these skills: Listening, Vocabulary, Grammar, Pronunciation, Speaking. They will help you reach your goal.*

A (10 minutes)

1. Say each phrase in the box and have students repeat.

2. Put students in pairs or small groups to complete the activity and discuss their answers.

3. Call on volunteers to share their ideas with the class. Ask questions: *What activities do you like? Do you have a favorite book? Are movies a good topic? What things are not good topics?*

Activity A Answers, p. 3
Answers will vary.

MULTILEVEL OPTION

Pair lower-level students with higher-level students to think of an example of each topic (for example, *Harry Potter,* basketball, brother, accountant, Seoul). Elicit examples from the class to check that students understand the vocabulary in Activity A.

B (5 minutes)

1. Focus students' attention on the photo. Have a volunteer describe the photo to the class. Read the question aloud.

2. Ask additional questions: *What is he building? Do you like it? Are you interested in building models like this?*

Activity B Answers, p. 3
Answers will vary. Possible answers: Building. He's building. He's building a model.

C (15 minutes)

1. Introduce the Unit Question: "What are you interested in?" Ask related information questions or questions about personal experience: *Do you like movies? Sports? Music? Are you interested in news or politics? What things are fun for you? What are you excited about?* Remind students to draw on their answers from Activities A and B.

2. Say the Unit Question again: "What are you interested in?" Seat students in small groups and direct them to pass around a paper as quickly as they can with each group member adding one item to the list. Tell them they have two minutes to make the lists, and they should write as many words as possible.

3. Call time and ask a reporter from each group to read the list aloud.

4. Use items from the lists as a springboard for discussion. For example, *Let's talk about books. What are your favorite books? Think about jobs. What jobs are you interested in?*

Activity C Answers, p. 3
Answers will vary. Possible answers: Sports. I like movies. I'm interested in art.

The Q Classroom

🔊 CD1, Track 2

1. Play *The Q Classroom*. Use the example from the audio to help students continue the conversation. Ask: *What did the students say? What are they interested in?*

2. To help students relate the conversation to their own experience, ask: *Do the students like the same things you do? Who is the most like you?*

▶ *Listening and Speaking Intro, page 4*

LISTENING

LISTENING: Are You Interested in Art?

VOCABULARY

A (10 minutes)

1. Go over the directions and the definitions in the box.

2. Direct students to circle the correct word or phrase to complete the sentences.

3. Put students in pairs to compare their answers.

4. Go over the answers with the class.

> **MULTILEVEL OPTION**
>
> Group lower-level students and assist them with the task. Provide alternate example sentences to help them understand the words. For example: *I **belong to** a book club. We read books and discuss them at meetings./My sister **collects** baseball caps. She has one from more than 50 teams./Mike is **good at** biology. He gets good grades in his biology classes./I'm not a basketball player, but I'm **interested in** the sport. I watch it on TV.*
>
> Have higher-level students complete the activity individually and then compare their answers with a partner. Tell the pairs to write an additional example conversation for each word or phrase. Have volunteers write one of their conversations on the board. Correct the conversations with the whole class, focusing on the use of the vocabulary rather than on other grammatical issues.

> **Activity A Answers, pp. 4–5**
> **1.** belong to   **2.** good at
> **3.** instrument   **4.** team
> **5.** hobbies   **6.** club
> **7.** collect   **8.** interested in

B (5 minutes)

1. Go over the directions.

2. Have students circle *T* or *F* and rewrite any *F* sentences to make them true.

3. Put students in pairs to compare and discuss their answers. Call on students to share their ideas with the class.

> **Activity B Answers, p. 5**
> Answers will vary. Possible answers:
> **1.** F; I don't collect coins.
> **2.** T; I belong to a cooking club.
> **3.** F; I'm not interested in sports.
> **4.** F; I'm good at math.
> **5.** F; My hobbies are tennis and painting.

PREVIEW THE LISTENING (5 minutes)

1. Direct students to look at the pictures. Ask: *Who do you see? Where are they?*

2. Read the sentences in Preview the Listening aloud. Have students match the sentences to the pictures.

3. Tell students they should review their answers after listening.

> **Preview the Listening Answers, p. 5**
> **1.** c;   **2.** a;   **3.** b

Listening Background Note

Some of the most popular free-time activities around the world are reading, watching TV, spending time with friends and family, using the computer, and exercising/working out.

Comprehension Check (20 minutes)

🔊 CD1, Track 3

A (10 minutes)

1. Go over the directions. Have students read the statements or read them aloud to the class.

2. Play the audio and have students complete the activity individually.

3. Have students compare answers with a partner. If necessary, play the audio again.

> **Activity A Answers, p. 6**
> **a.** T;   **b.** F;   **c.** F

B (10 minutes)

1. Go over the directions and the activities in the chart.

2. As you play the audio, have students listen and check the activities next to each speaker.

3. Have students compare their answers with a partner.

4. Replay the audio so that partners can check their answers.

5. Go over the answers with the class.

> **Activity B Answers, p. 6**
> **1.** Lin: hiking, movies, art; James: movies, art
> **2.** David: comic books, soccer; Anna: books, soccer
> **3.** Sam: soccer, tennis; Mika: guitar, tennis

C (10 minutes)

1. Go over the directions.

2. Have students read the sentences. Then play the audio again and have students complete the activity individually.

3. Have students compare their answers with a partner.

4. Go over the answers with the class.

> **Activity C Answers, p. 6**
> **1.** a. weekend; b. movie
> **2.** a. twelve; b. soccer
> **3.** a. piano; b. tennis

EXPANSION ACTIVITY: Create Conversations
(15–20 minutes)

1. Put students in pairs to create their own conversations. If helpful, play the audio again so that students can follow the models.

2. Have each pair choose a situation: two students meeting in class for the first time, two friends talking about activities, two students sitting outside who know each other a little bit.

3. Have students write out the conversation. Walk around the room to provide help as needed.

4. Ask volunteers to perform their conversations in front of the class.

▶ *Listening and Speaking Intro, page 7*

Building Vocabulary: Collocations for hobbies and interests (10 minutes)

1. Direct students to read the information.

2. Check students' comprehension of the information. Say a verb and elicit a noun or a preposition + noun collocation. For example, say: *be good at (sports); go (shopping/hiking).*

Skill Note

Knowing collocations can help students speak more fluently. They should try to remember a phrase, not each word. Students can keep a list of collocations in a vocabulary notebook. This will help them learn the collocations. When you introduce vocabulary in class, suggest collocations for the words. Have students notice the words around a new word in a sentence.

A (10 minutes)
CD1, Track 4

1. Go over the directions.

2. Direct students to read the paragraph and complete the sentences with collocations.

3. Have students compare their answers with a partner.

4. Play the audio and have students check their answers.

5. Go over the answers with the class.

> **Activity A Answers, p. 7**
> **1.** in **2.** in **3.** at **4.** play
> **5.** take **6.** ride **7.** go **8.** to
> **9.** watch **10.** play **11.** go
> **12.** together **13.** read

▶ *Listening and Speaking Intro, page 8*

B (10 minutes)
CD1, Track 5

1. Go over the directions.

2. Play the audio and have students complete the activity individually.

3. Have students compare their answers with a partner. If necessary, play the audio again.

4. Go over the answers with the class.

> **Activity B Answers, p. 8**
> **1.** Sun Hee reads books. She is interested in sports.
> **2.** Khalid plays video games. He rides his bike on weekends.

C (10 minutes)

1. Go over the directions.

2. Have students write five sentences about themselves.

3. Put students in pairs or small groups to read their sentences aloud.

Activity C Answers, p. 8
Answers will vary. Possible answers:
I'm interested in music.
I play video games on weekends.
I watch movies and television.
I'm good at tennis.
I go shopping with my friends.

MULTILEVEL OPTION

Have higher-level students work with lower-level students to create sentences. If necessary, suggest the lower-level student dictate ideas to their higher-level partner. The lower-level student can use the partner's sentences as a guide.

 For additional practice with collocations for hobbies and interests, have students visit *Q Online Practice*.

WHAT DO YOU THINK?

A (15 minutes)
1. Go over the directions.
2. Read each question aloud and have students repeat.
3. Model the activity. Call on a student and ask the first question. If the student answers *yes*, pretend to write the name in the book.
4. Have students stand and walk around the room asking and answering the questions.

Activity A Answers, p. 8
Answers will vary.

Tip for Success (1 minute)
1. Read the tip aloud.
2. Encourage students to use *too* in Activity B.

B (5 minutes)
1. Go over the directions and the example.
2. Have students share their answers to Activity A in small groups.
3. Call on students to tell the class about one person they talked to.

Activity B Answers, p. 8
Answers will vary.

Learning Outcome

Use the Learning Outcome to frame the purpose and relevance of the Listening. Say: *The Learning Outcome is to interview someone about the things they are interested in and the things they are good at. What did you learn from the Listening? How will it help you describe a classmate's interests and abilities?*

(Students learned to use collocations for hobbies and interests.)

▶ *Listening and Speaking Intro, page 9*

SPEAKING

Grammar: Present of *be*; Simple present affirmative statements (10 minutes)

1. Read the statement about when the present of *be* is used.
2. Focus students' attention on the charts on p. 9. Go over how to form affirmative and negative sentences with the present of *be*.
3. Say and have students repeat the sentences.
4. Go over the information about contractions and questions with *be*.
5. Provide and elicit additional examples for both charts: *I am a teacher. You are not from the United States. We are in class now. Your parents aren't old. He isn't good at painting. Are they good at chess? Yes, they are.*

Tip for Success (1 minute)
1. Read the tip aloud.
2. Emphasize that the statements in the chart are examples of the parts of speech that follow the verb *be*.

▶ *Listening and Speaking Intro, page 10*
1. Read the information about information questions on p. 10.
2. Focus students' attention on the charts. Say and have students repeat the sentences.
3. Read the statements and examples about when the simple present is used. Provide and elicit additional examples for each situation. For example, habits: *They see a movie every Thursday.*
4. Ask questions from the charts or use other examples: *Are you interested in sports? Is your sister good at cooking? Where are you from?* Elicit answers from students.

5. Check comprehension by asking questions: *What form of* be *do we use with* they? *What is the contraction for* they are not? *What kind of word is first in an information question? What does the simple present describe?*

Skill Note

Students are often hesitant to use contractions because they think they are too informal or because they aren't sure exactly how to say them. Encourage students to practice using contractions. If they say the full form, ask them to repeat using the contracted form.

Students also have trouble remembering the *-s* ending on the verb used with *he, she,* or *it.* Point out that if the listener doesn't hear the *-s* ending, he or she may not understand or will think the speaker doesn't speak English very well. Have students exaggerate the sound as they make present affirmative statements.

A (15 minutes)

1. Go over the directions. Have students work individually to put the words in the correct order to make questions.

2. Have students compare their questions with a partner. Go over the questions with the class.

3. Have students take turns asking and answering the questions in pairs. Direct them to write their partner's answers on the lines.

4. Call on students to share their partner's answers with the class.

> **Activity A Answers, pp. 10–11**
> Partner's answers will vary.
> **2.** Are you interested in art?
> **3.** What are you good at?
> **4.** Are you 20 years old?
> **5.** Are you on a team?

▶ *Listening and Speaking Intro, page 11*

B (15 minutes)

1. Have students complete the activity individually, then compare their answers with a partner.

2. Go over the answers with the class.

3. Have students practice the conversations in pairs.

> **Activity B Answers, p. 11**
> **1.** are; go; take
> **2.** Is; is; belongs
> **3.** Are; 're not/aren't/are not; are/'re; live
> **4.** Are; play; am not/'m not; plays; belong
> **5.** Are; are; go
> **6.** is, listens

 For additional practice with the present of *be* and simple present affirmative statements, have students visit *Q Online Practice.*

MULTILEVEL OPTION

Have lower-level students work in pairs to complete the conversations. Have higher-level students write two more conversations and then share them with a partner.

▶ *Listening and Speaking Intro, page 12*

Pronunciation: Simple present third-person *-s/-es* (5 minutes)

◉ CD1, Track 6

1. Read the information about simple present third-person *-s/-es.*

2. Play the audio.

3. Check comprehension by asking questions: *What sound does* s *make at the end of the verb* get? *What does* s *sound like after* listen? *What is the sound for the -es ending?*

Skill Note

When a word ends with a voiceless consonant sound (*f, k, p, t*), the *-s* sounds like /s/. When the word ends in a vowel sound (*play*), or with a voiced consonant sound (*b, d, g, m, n, r, v*), the *s* sounds like /z/. When the word ends in a sound that is close to an *s* sound (*ch, sh, s, x, z, j,* soft *g*), the ending is a new syllable and sounds like /ɪz/.

Suggest that students put their hands on their throats as they say these words: *take, get, live, move, work, walk, clap, run, read.* Have them notice which words make their throats vibrate (*live, move, run, read*). Adding an *-s* will sound like a /z/ on those words.

A (10 minutes)

◉ CD1 Track 7

1. Go over the directions.

2. Play the audio and have students circle the correct sound.

3. Have students compare their answers with a partner.

4. Play the audio again so students can check their answers.

5. Go over the answers with the class.

Activity A Answers, p. 12
1. /z/ **2.** /s/
3. /z/ **4.** /ɪz/
5. /s/ **6.** /z/
7. /ɪz/ **8.** /z/

Critical Thinking Tip (1 minute)

1. Read the tip aloud.
2. Point out that being able to identify the difference in sounds at the end of verbs will help students with spelling.

Critical Q:Expansion Activity

Identify

1. For more practice with identifying these sounds, play the audio for Building Vocabulary: Collocations, Activity A on p. 7.
2. With their books closed, have students write verbs they hear that have one of the -s/-es ending sounds and identify the word and which sound it makes (e.g., *lives, works, sings*).
3. Elicit answers from the class.
4. As a challenge, suggest students go online and search for "news in English" to find an audio program (possible sources: npr, bbc, abcnews, nbcnews, cnn).
5. Have students listen to five minutes of audio and write down any verbs with the -s/-es ending sound that they can identify.
6. Elicit examples from the class.

B (10 minutes)

1. Go over the directions.
2. Say the verbs in the box and have students repeat.
3. Have students work individually to complete the activity.

Activity B Answers, p. 12
Answers will vary. Possible answers:
1. May goes hiking every Friday.
2. Tom plays the guitar.
3. Mario belongs to the tennis team.
4. Anna watches movies with her friends.
5. Jing gets together with friends every night.

C (5 minutes)

1. Go over the directions.
2. Have students work in pairs. One person says the sentences as the other circles the sound. Then they change roles.

3. Call on students to read their sentences to the class. Elicit the sound.

Activity C Answers, p. 12
Answers will vary.

 For additional practice with simple present third-person -s/-es, have students visit *Q Online Practice*.

Listening and Speaking Intro, page 13
Speaking Skill: Keeping a conversation going *Part 1* (5 minutes)

CD1, Track 8
1. Direct students to read about adding extra information to answers. Play the audio example conversations.
2. Check comprehension: *What extra information does Speaker B add about Bangkok? About cooking?*

Tip for Success (1 minute)

1. Read the tip aloud.
2. Point out that it is not necessary to ask a long question to keep a conversation going. Questions encourage people to continue talking, especially if they are about themselves, for instance: *How about you?*

Speaking Skill Activity (10 minutes)

1. Go over the directions of the activity.
2. Model the activity with a student. Ask: *What are your hobbies?* Elicit more information (for example, *I like sports. Basketball is my favorite*).
3. Direct students to write answers to the questions.
4. Have students work in pairs to take turns asking and answering the questions.
5. Call on students to ask a classmate a question.

Speaking Skill Activity Answers, p. 13
Answers will vary. Possible answers:
1. My hobbies are art and basketball. I belong to the basketball team.
2. I like soccer, too. I play soccer on the weekends.
3. I'm good at cooking. I cook for my friends sometimes.
4. *Avatar* is my favorite movie, too. It's exciting!
5. Yes, I am. I go to the museum with my family.
6. I'm interested in music. Jazz is my favorite.

Speaking Skill: Keeping a conversation going *Part 2* (5 minutes)

 CD1, Track 9

1. Direct student to read the information about taking time to think.
2. Play the audio examples.
3. Check comprehension. Ask: *What expressions show that you are thinking?*

A (10 minutes)

 CD1 Track 10

1. Play the audio and have students complete the activity individually.
2. Have students check their answers with a partner. Play the audio again if necessary.
3. Go over the answers with the class.
4. Have students practice the conversations in pairs.

> **Activity A Answers, p. 14**
> **1.** Uh
> **2.** Hmm
> **3.** Let me see
> **4.** Well
> **5.** Let me think
> **6.** Well

B (10 minutes)

1. Go over the directions and the example conversation.
2. Have students practice the conversations in pairs.

> **Activity B Answers, p. 14**
> Answers will vary.

 For additional practice with keeping a conversation going, have students visit *Q Online Practice*.

Unit Assignment: Interview and introduce a classmate

Unit Question (5 minutes)

Refer students back to the ideas they discussed at the beginning of the unit about hobbies and interests. Provide or elicit examples they wrote on their lists (e.g., books, movies, jobs, sports). Cue students if necessary by asking specific questions about the content of the unit: *What are some hobbies and interests you have? What are some expressions for hobbies and interests?*

Learning Outcome

1. Tie the Unit Assignment to the unit Learning Outcome. Say: *The outcome for this unit is to interview a classmate about his or her interests and introduce him or her to the class. This Unit Assignment is going to let you introduce a classmate and describe his or her hobbies and interests.*

2. Explain that you are going to use a rubric similar to their Self-Assessment checklist on p. 16 to grade their Unit Assignment. You can also share a copy of the Unit Assignment Rubric (on p. 10 of this *Teacher's Handbook*) with the students.

Consider the Ideas

A (5 minutes)

1. Go over the directions. Say each item and have students repeat.
2. Direct students to check the appropriate boxes.
3. Go over the answers with the class.

> **Activity A Answers, p. 15**
> Checked: a greeting, country, job, favorite movie, hobbies and interests, name

B (5 minutes)

 CD1, Track 11

1. Go over the directions.
2. Play the audio and have students complete the activity individually.
3. Go over the answers with the class.

> **Activity B Answers, p. 15**
> Circled: a greeting, country, job, favorite movie, hobbies and interests, name

Prepare and Speak

Gather Ideas

A (10 minutes)

1. Go over the directions, the steps, and the questions in the questionnaire on p. 16.
2. Have students add one question.
3. Direct students to work in pairs to ask and answer the questions so that each partner has a completed questionnaire.

4. Remind students to give extra information in their answers and to use expressions that show they are thinking about their answers.

▶ *Listening and Speaking Intro, page 16*

Organize Ideas

B (10 minutes)

1. Go over the directions.
2. Direct students to write five or six sentences about their partners.

21ST CENTURY SKILLS

Being able to interview someone else is a skill students will need in both professional and academic settings. Remembering key information and communicating it to others is an essential communicative function in the business world.

Speak

Tip for Success (1 minute)

1. Read the tip aloud.
2. Remind students to speak clearly when they introduce their partners.

C (15 minutes)

1. Have students review the Self-Assessment checklist on p. 16 and note what they should include in their introductions. Suggest students speak slowly and in a loud enough voice to be clear.
2. Suggest students review the vocabulary on p. 4 and the collocations on p. 7. Students can review the present of *be* and simple present statements on pp. 9 and 10.
3. Have students introduce their partners to the class.
4. Use the Unit Assignment Rubric on p. 10 of this *Teacher's Handbook* to score each student's introduction.
5. Alternatively, divide the class into large groups and have students introduce their partners to their group. Have listeners complete the Unit Assignment Rubric.

Check and Reflect

Check

A (5 minutes)

1. Direct students to read and complete the Self-Assessment checklist.
2. Ask for a show of hands for how many students gave all or mostly *yes* answers.
3. Congratulate them on their success. Discuss the steps they can take if an item on the checklist was difficult for them. For example, if they had trouble using the vocabulary from the unit, they can try practicing those words over the next week.

▶ *Listening and Speaking Intro, page 17*

Reflect

B (5 minutes)

1. Direct students to discuss the questions with a partner.
2. Elicit ideas from the class.
3. Ask students if the unit prepared them to introduce a classmate.

Track Your Success

1. Have students circle the words they have learned in this unit. Suggest that students go back through the unit to review any words they have forgotten.
2. Have students check the skills they have mastered. If students need more practice to feel confident about their proficiency in a skill, point out the page numbers and encourage them to review.
3. Read the Learning Outcome aloud. Ask students if they feel that they have met the outcome.

Unit Assignment Rubric

Student name: _____

Date: _____

Unit Assignment: *Interview and introduce a classmate.*

20 points = Introduction element was completely successful (at least 90% of the time).
15 points = Introduction element was mostly successful (at least 70% of the time).
10 points = Introduction element was partially successful (at least 50% of the time).
  0 points = Introduction element was not successful.

Make an introduction	20 points	15 points	10 points	0 points
Student's introduction was clear.				
Student used vocabulary from this unit.				
Student used the verb *be* correctly.				
Student used simple present statements correctly.				
Student included interesting information about partner.				

Total points: _____

Comments:

Unit QUESTION

How do you make friends?

Friendship

LISTENING • listening for examples
VOCABULARY • word categories
GRAMMAR • simple present
PRONUNCIATION • sentence intonation
SPEAKING • adding more information

LEARNING OUTCOME

Give a presentation that describes some good ways to make friends, including details and examples.

▶ *Listening and Speaking Intro, page 19*

Preview the Unit

Learning Outcome

1. Ask for a volunteer to read the unit skills and then the unit Learning Outcome.

2. Explain: *Your goal for the unit is to be able to give a presentation that describes some good ways to make friends. I will use this Learning Outcome to grade your work at the end of the unit. Focus on learning these skills: Listening, Vocabulary, Grammar, Pronunciation, Speaking. They will help you reach your goal.*

A (10 minutes)

1. Prepare students for thinking about the topic by telling them about an activity in which you met a friend.

2. Put students in pairs or small groups to complete the activity and discuss their answers.

3. Call on volunteers to share their ideas with the class. Ask questions: *What activities are good for talking to people? What activities are good to do alone?*

Activity A Answers, p. 19
Answers will vary.

MULTILEVEL OPTION

Have higher-level students work in pairs to add five other activities that are good for making friends.

B (5 minutes)

1. Focus students' attention on the photo. Have a volunteer describe the photo to the class. Read the question aloud.

2. Ask additional questions: *Do you like chess? Do people play chess in parks near you? Is it more fun when it's big like this?*

Activity B Answers, p. 19
Answers will vary. Possible answers: Chess. They're playing chess. They're playing chess in a park.

C (15 minutes)

1. Introduce the Unit Question: "How do you make friends?" Ask related information questions or questions about personal experience: *Where do you meet people? How do you start a conversation? What things do you do with your friends?* Remind students to draw on their answers from Activities A and B.

2. Label four pieces of poster paper (*Activities, Work, School, Other*) and place them in the corners of the room.

3. Ask students to read and consider the Unit Question for a moment and then to stand in the corner next to the poster that best represents their answer to the question.

4. Direct the groups in each corner to talk among themselves about the reasons for their answer. Tell them to choose a secretary to record the answers on the poster paper.

5. Call on volunteers from each corner to share their opinions with the class.

6. Leave the posters up for students to refer to at the end of the unit.

Activity C Answers, p. 19
Answers will vary. Possible answers: School. At school. I make friends at school.

The Q Classroom

CD1, Track 12

1. Play *The Q Classroom*. Use the example from the audio to help students continue the conversation. Ask: *What did the students say? The students list some activities they do. What are they? The teacher says we can make friends through activities and something else. What else does she say helps us make friends?*
2. Have students talk in pairs about which students from *The Q classroom* have the best ideas.

▶ *Listening and Speaking Intro, page 20*

Listening

LISTENING: Making Friends

VOCABULARY

A (10 minutes)

1. Go over the directions.
2. Direct students to circle the answer that best matches the meaning of each bold word.
3. Put students in pairs to compare their answers.
4. Go over the answers with the class.

Tip for Success (1 minute)

1. Read the tip aloud.
2. Suggest students write the new vocabulary words in their notebooks, including which part of speech each word is.
3. Help with identifying parts of speech, e.g., *advice* = noun, *join* = verb, *positive* = adjective.

MULTILEVEL OPTION

Allow lower-level students to use their dictionaries. Have higher-level students complete the activity individually and then compare their answers with a partner. Tell the pairs to write a story using all eight vocabulary words. For example: *My friend is a **volunteer** at a library....* Ask volunteers to tell their stories to the class. Have listeners write the vocabulary words in the order they hear them.

Activity A Answers, p. 20

1. b
2. a
3. b
4. b
5. a
6. a
7. b
8. a

Critical Thinking Tip (1 minute)

1. Read the tip aloud.
2. Point out that in this activity, students may not know the target vocabulary, but if they know all or most of the other words in the sentences, that will help them choose the best answer.

▶ *Listening and Speaking Intro, page 21*

B (10 minutes)

1. Go over the directions.
2. Direct students to complete the activity individually.
3. Have students compare their answers with a partner.
4. Go over the answers with the class.

Activity B Answers, p. 21

1. join
2. compliments
3. close
4. volunteer
5. share
6. positive

web+ For additional practice with the vocabulary, have students visit *Q Online Practice.*

PREVIEW THE LISTENING (5 minutes)

1. Go over the directions.
2. Have students match the names to the pictures.
3. Tell students they should review their answers after listening.

Preview the Listening Answers, p. 21
1. b; **2.** a; **3.** c

Critical Q: Expansion Activity

Define

1. Put students in pairs. Give each pair one new word (*encourage, personality, patient, outgoing, shy, helpful, honest, similar, peer*).
2. Have students use their dictionaries to find the meaning of the word and then write three sentences which use the word.
3. Have each pair exchange sentences with another pair who will read the sentences and write a possible definition for the word (without using their dictionaries).
4. Have students check their ideas with the other pair.

Listening Background Note

The first speaker is a teacher at a college. College is another name for university in the United States. Community colleges are two years, but other colleges are four years.

 Listening and Speaking Intro, page 22

Comprehension Check

CD1, Track 13

A (10 minutes)

1. Go over the directions. Read each piece of advice aloud and have students repeat.
2. Play the audio and have students complete the activity individually.
3. Have students compare their answers with a partner. If helpful, play the audio again.
4. Go over the answers with the class.

> **Activity A Answers, p. 22**
> **1b.** T
> **2a.** T
> **2b.** F; David has breakfast with friends on Saturdays.
> **3a.** F; Dr. Johnson and Rob are not close friends.
> **3b.** F; Dr. Johnson has advice for shy people.

B (10 minutes)

1. Go over the directions.
2. Have students read the statements.
3. Play the audio and have students complete the activity individually.
4. Go over the answers with the class.

> **Activity B Answers, p. 22**
> **1.** b. T
> **2.** a. T, b. T
> **3.** a. F, b. F

EXPANSION ACTIVITY: Listen for Information
(10 minutes)

1. Play the audio for Activity B again and have students take notes on other information they hear.
2. Have students write two questions about each conversation.
3. Put students in pairs and have them take turns asking and answering their questions.

Building Vocabulary: Word categories
(5 minutes)

1. Direct students to read the information silently.
2. Check comprehension: *What is a category? What category do* piano *and* guitar *belong to?*

Skill Note

Point out that using categories expands vocabulary in two ways: Students can add other related items to the group, and they can learn the category name. This can help them to remember or explain new words better.

▶ *Listening and Speaking Intro, page 23*

A (10 minutes)

1. Go over the directions and the categories in the chart. Say each word in the box and have students repeat.
2. Have students work individually to write the words in the chart. Have students add two words to each category.
3. Have students compare their answers with a partner.
4. Go over the answers with the class.

> **Activity A Answers, p. 23**
> Music: classical, French, rock, Spanish
> Hobbies: chess, cooking, reading, video games, skiing, tennis, volleyball
> Classes: biology, math, Spanish, cooking, French, history
> Sports: skiing, tennis, volleyball

B (5 minutes)

🔊 CD1, Track 14

1. Go over the directions. Say each word and have students repeat.
2. Play the audio and have students complete the activity individually.
3. Have students compare their answers with a partner.
4. Go over the answers with the class.

> **Activity B Answers, p. 23**
> Music: folk, blues
> Hobbies: chorus
> Classes: calculus, physics
> Sports: lacrosse, rugby, racquetball

C (5 minutes)

1. Go over the directions.
2. Direct students to complete the conversations with their own ideas.
3. Elicit ideas from the class.
4. Have students practice the conversations in pairs.

> **Activity C Answers, p. 23**
> Answers will vary. Possible answers:
> **1.** jazz
> **2.** pizza
> **3.** baseball
> **4.** flute

 For additional practice with word categories, have students visit *Q Online Practice*.

▶ *Listening and Speaking Intro, page 24*

Listening Skill: Listening for examples
(5 minutes)

🔊 CD1, Track 15

1. Play the audio and have students read along silently.
2. Check comprehension by asking questions: *What words introduce examples? Where does* like *come in the sentence? Where can* for example *come?*

A (10 minutes)

🔊 CD1, Track 16

1. Go over the directions.
2. Play the audio and have students complete the activity individually.
3. Have students compare their answers in pairs. If necessary, play the audio again.
4. Go over the answers with the class.
5. Have students read the conversation in pairs.

> **Activity A Answers, p. 24**
> **1.** chess
> **2.** French, Spanish
> **3.** movies, classes
> **4.** a coffee shop, the library

B (5 minutes)

🔊 CD1, Track 17

1. Play the audio and have students circle the word(s) they hear.
2. Have students compare their answers in pairs.
3. Go over the answers with the class.

> **Activity B Answers, p. 24**
> **1.** like
> **2.** for example
> **3.** like
> **4.** like

 For additional practice with listening for examples, have students visit *Q Online Practice*.

WHAT DO YOU THINK?

A (5 minutes)

1. Go over the directions and the items. Say each item and have students repeat.
2. Have students complete the activity individually.

> **Activity A Answers, p. 24**
> Answers will vary.

B (5 minutes)

1. Go over the directions and the example.
2. Put students in pairs to talk about three things they do to meet people.
3. Call on each pair or group to share their answers with the class.

Learning Outcome

Use the Learning Outcome to frame the purpose and relevance of the Listening. Say: *The Learning Outcome is to give a presentation describing some good ways to make friends. What did you learn from the Listening? How will it help you talk about good ways to make friends?*

(Students learned specific ideas for making friends.)

MULTILEVEL OPTION

Have lower-level students work in groups to make a list of three additional tips on how to make new friends. They can refer to a dictionary if they wish. Have higher-level students work in pairs to make a list of ten tips on how to make new friends. The list can include more places to meet people and also how to behave. Have students present their ideas to the class.

▶ *Listening and Speaking Intro, page 25*

SPEAKING

Grammar: Simple present (10 minutes)

1. Read the introductory information and the bullet points about the simple present.
2. Say each sentence and have students repeat.
3. Check comprehension by asking questions: *How do you make a negative sentence? What is the first word in a* yes/no *question? What is the first word in a* wh- *question?*

Skill Note

Students often have trouble with the *-s/-es* ending for *he, she,* and *it.* They often drop it completely, but they may also add it to the main verb even in questions and negative statements. Use the board to write affirmative statements with the subjects *he, she,* and *it.* Underline or use colors to emphasize the *-s/-es* ending. Change the affirmative statement to a question and then to the negative. Use underlining or colors to show the *-es* ending on *does.*

Tip for Success (1 minute)

1. Read the tip aloud.
2. Call on students and ask information questions. Elicit short answers.

▶ *Listening and Speaking Intro, page 26*

A (10 minutes)

1. Go over the directions.
2. Have students complete the activity individually.
3. Have students compare their answers with a partner.
4. Go over the answers with the class.
5. Have students practice the conversations in pairs.

Activity A Answers, p. 26
1. How often do you see; don't see; Does he play; does; play
2. share; belong; Where do you go; go; Do you want
3. like; Where do you shop; buy, don't cost; love, works

B (10 minutes)

1. Go over the directions.
2. Have students complete the activity individually.
3. Have students compare their answers with a partner.
4. Go over the answers with the class.

Activity B Answers, p. 26
2. What do the volunteers do?
3. Shy people don't talk a lot.
4. Does the class begin at 3:00?
5. Do you like video games?
6. She doesn't listen to rock music.

▶ *Listening and Speaking Intro, page 27*

C (10 minutes)

1. Go over the directions.
2. Model the activity. Elicit the correct order for the first question and write it on the board. Remind students to put the *wh-* word first for information questions and *do* or *does* first for *yes/no* questions.
3. Have students complete the activity individually.
4. Have students compare their answers with a partner.
5. Go over the answers with the class.
6. Have students work in pairs and have them take turns asking and answering the questions.
7. Call on students to share their partner's answers with the class.

Activity C Answers, p. 27
Partner's answers will vary. Possible answers:
1. Where do you usually meet people?
   I usually meet people at school.
2. Do you know people on your street?
   Yes, I do.
3. What do you do with your friends?
   We see movies together.
4. Where do you go with your friends?
   We go to the mall.
5. Answers will vary. Possible answers: Do you meet people in coffee shops?
   No, I don't.

 For additional practice with the simple present, have students visit *Q Online Practice*.

MULTILEVEL OPTION

Have lower-level students work together to write the questions and the answers. Have higher-level students write a paragraph about their partner's answers.

Pronunciation: Sentence intonation
(5 minutes)

🔊 CD1, Track 18

1. Read the information about sentence intonation.
2. Play the audio.
3. Check comprehension by asking questions: *Does your voice go up or down at the end of statements? Does your voice go up or down at the end of* yes/ no *questions? Does your voice go up or down at the end of information questions? What word means* go down?

▶ *Listening and Speaking Intro, page 28*

A (10 minutes)
🔊 CD1, Track 19

1. Go over the directions.
2. Play the audio and have students circle the answers.
3. Have students compare their answers in pairs. If necessary, play the audio again.
4. Go over the answers with the class.
5. Play the audio again and have students repeat.

Activity A Answers, p. 28
1. rising
2. falling
3. rising
4. falling
5. falling
6. rising
7. falling
8. falling
9. falling
10. falling

B (5 minutes)
1. Go over the directions.
2. Have students work in pairs to practice the conversations.
3. Call on students to share their partner's answers with the class.

Activity B Answers, p. 28
Answers will vary.

 For additional practice with sentence intonation, have students visit *Q Online Practice*.

Unit Assignment: Give a presentation about good ways to make friends

Unit Question (5 minutes)

Refer students back to the ideas they discussed at the beginning of the unit about meeting people and making friends. Cue students if necessary by asking specific questions about the content of the unit: *What are good ways to meet people? How do people make friends? What are good things to talk about?* Go over the Unit Assignment.

Learning Outcome

1. Tie the Unit Assignment to the unit Learning Outcome. Say: *The outcome for this unit is to give a presentation that describes some good ways to make friends. This Unit Assignment is going to let you show your skill in giving a presentation.*

2. Explain that you are going to use a rubric similar to their Self-Assessment checklist on p. 30 to grade their Unit Assignment. You can also share a copy of the Unit Assignment Rubric (on p. 19 of this *Teacher's Handbook*) with the students.

Consider the Ideas (15 minutes)

🔊 CD1, Track 20

1. Go over the directions.
2. Play the audio and have students complete the activity individually.
3. Go over the answers with the class.

> **Consider the Ideas Answers, p. 28**
> Answers will vary. Possible answers:
> **1.** work at the food bank, read to children at the library
> **2.** movie, Spanish, chess
> **3.** soccer, swimming, lacrosse
> **4.** art, cooking

▶ *Listening and Speaking Intro, page 29*

Prepare and Speak

Gather Ideas

A (10 minutes)

1. Go over the directions, example conversation, and steps.
2. Elicit other ideas besides those in the box.
3. Model the conversation with three volunteers.
4. Put students in groups of four to complete the chart.
5. Walk around the room to provide help as needed.

Tip for Success (1 minute)

1. Read the tip aloud.
2. Encourage students to use examples in their conversations.

▶ *Listening and Speaking Intro, page 30*

Skill Review: Adding information
(5 minutes)

1. Go over the information.
2. If necessary, have students refer to the skill box on p. 13.
3. Point out that adding information will help them give a better presentation on good ways to make friends.

4. Go over the steps. Say the sentences in steps 3 and 4 so students can practice.
5. Have students follow the steps to prepare their presentations.

Organize Ideas

B (15–20 minutes)

1. Go over the directions, the steps, and the questions in the questionnaire on p. 16.
2. Have students add one question.
3. Direct students to work in pairs to ask and answer the questions so that each partner has a completed questionnaire.
4. Remind students to give extra information in their answers and to use expressions that show they are thinking about their answers.

Tip for Success (1 minute)

1. Read the tip aloud.
2. Allow enough time for students to practice their presentations two or three times.

Speak

C (20 minutes)

1. Go over the directions.
2. Have students review the Self-Assessment checklist on p. 30 to note what they should include in their presentations. Go over each point and discuss what it means. Suggest students review sections of the unit if necessary: to use vocabulary from the unit, look at p. 20; to use the simple present correctly, look at p. 25; to give examples, look at p. 24.
3. Have groups give their presentations to the class.
4. Use the Unit Assignment Rubric on p. 19 of this *Teacher's Handbook* to score each student's presentation.
5. Alternatively, divide the class into large groups and have students give their presentations to their group. Have listeners complete the Unit Assignment Rubric.

Students will have to make presentations on a range of topics in their academic and professional lives. Making effective presentations requires good preparation, clear ideas, and the ability to express oneself. In this assignment, students also have to work together to plan and implement the presentation.

Check and Reflect

Check

A (5 minutes)

1. Direct students to read and complete the Self-Assessment checklist.

2. Ask for a show of hands for how many students gave all or mostly *yes* answers.

3. Congratulate them on their success. Discuss the steps they can take if an item on the checklist was difficult for them. For example, if they had trouble using the simple present correctly, suggest they try using it in conversations over the next week.

▶ *Listening and Speaking Intro, page 31*

Reflect

B (5 minutes)

1. Go over the directions. Read the questions aloud.

2. Direct students to discuss the questions with a partner.

3. Elicit ideas from the class.

Track Your Success

1. Have students circle the words they have learned in this unit. Suggest that students go back through the unit to review any words they have forgotten.

2. Have students check the skills they have mastered. If students need more practice to feel confident about their proficiency in a skill, point out the page numbers and encourage them to review.

3. Read the Learning Outcome aloud. Ask students if they feel that they have met the outcome.

Unit 2 Friendship

Unit Assignment Rubric

Student name: _____

Date: _____

Unit Assignment: *Give a presentation on good ways to make friends.*

20 points = Presentation element was completely successful (at least 90% of the time).
15 points = Presentation element was mostly successful (at least 70% of the time).
10 points = Presentation element was partially successful (at least 50% of the time).
  0 points = Presentation element was not successful.

Give a presentation on good ways to make friends	20 points	15 points	10 points	0 points
Student's part of presentation was clear.				
Student used vocabulary from the unit.				
Student used the simple present correctly.				
Student gave clear examples to help the audience understand.				
Student added information, such as details and examples.				

Total points: _____

Comments:

Unit QUESTION
What makes a good school?

Education

LISTENING • listening for examples
VOCABULARY • using the dictionary: antonyms
GRAMMAR • adjectives; adverbs + adjectives
PRONUNCIATION • sentence stress
SPEAKING • giving opinions

LEARNING OUTCOME

Share your opinions to plan a perfect school and present your plan to the class.

▶ *Listening and Speaking Intro, page 33*

Preview the Unit

Learning Outcome

1. Ask for a volunteer to read the unit skills and then the unit Learning Outcome.

2. Explain: *Your goal for the unit is to be able to share your opinions to plan a perfect school and present your plan to the class. I will use this Learning Outcome to grade your work at the end of the unit. Focus on learning these skills: Listening, Vocabulary, Grammar, Pronunciation, Speaking. They will help you reach your goal.*

A (10 minutes)

1. Put students in pairs or small groups to complete the activity and discuss their answers.

2. Call on volunteers to share their ideas with the class. Ask questions: *What is a good number of students to have in a school? What is a good number of students to have in a class? What do you like about this school?*

> **Activity A Answers, p. 33**
> Answers will vary.

MULTILEVEL OPTION

Group lower-level students to review vocabulary from Units 1 and 2 and brainstorm names of clubs and sports teams. Have higher-level students work in pairs to write three more questions about their school and answer them. Call on students to share their ideas with the class.

B (5 minutes)

1. Focus students' attention on the photo. Have a volunteer describe the photo to the class. Read the question aloud.

2. Ask additional questions: *Is this a large class? Do you have a class like this one? Do you like it?*

> **Activity B Answers, p. 33**
> Answers will vary. Possible answers: Science. They're in a science class. They're reading books and doing science experiments.

C (10 minutes)

1. Introduce the Unit Question: "What makes a good school?" Ask related information questions or questions about personal experience. Ask: *What do you like about this school? What do you like about other schools? Is size important? Are clubs and teams important?* Remind students to draw on their answers from Activities A and B.

2. Say the Unit Question again: "What makes a good school?" Seat students in small groups and direct them to pass around a paper as quickly as they can with each group member adding one item to the list. Tell them they have two minutes to make the lists, and that they should write as many words as possible.

3. Call time and ask a reporter from each group to read the list aloud.

4. Use items from the lists as a springboard for discussion. For example, *Let's talk about class size. What is a good number of students to have in a class?*

> **Activity C Answers, p. 33**
> Answers will vary. Possible answers:
> Good teachers. Good teachers and interesting classes. A good school has good teachers and interesting classes.

The Q Classroom

CD1, Track 21

1. Play *The Q Classroom*. Use the example from the audio to help students continue the conversation. Ask: *What did the students say? What did each of the four students like in a school?*

2. Have students give their own opinions. Ask: *Who do you agree with? What idea is not very important to you?*

▶ *Listening and Speaking Intro, page 34*

LISTENING

LISTENING: Let's Take a Tour

VOCABULARY

A (10 minutes)

1. Go over the directions.

2. Direct students to complete the activity individually.

3. Have students compare their answers with a partner.

4. Go over the answers with the class.

Tip for Success (1 minute)

1. Read the tip aloud.

2. Point out that *college* and *university* are institutions of higher learning, that is, beyond high school.

MULTILEVEL OPTION

Group lower-level students and assist them with the task. Provide alternate example sentences to help them understand the words. For example: *Students often have many places to eat on a university campus, like cafeterias, dining halls, and coffee shops. My mother cooks a **special** dinner on my birthday./Julia is a very **active** student. She belongs to five clubs./One of my **skills** is computer programming.*

Have higher-level students complete the activity individually and then compare their answers with a partner. Tell the pairs to write an additional sample sentence for each word or phrase. Have volunteers write one of their sentences on the board. Correct the sentences with the whole class, focusing on the use of the words rather than on other grammatical issues.

Activity A Answers, p. 34
1. a; **2.** b; **3.** b; **4.** a; **5.** a; **6.** a; **7.** b; **8.** b

▶ *Listening and Speaking Intro, page 35*

B (10 minutes)

1. Go over the directions.

2. Direct students to complete the activity individually.

3. Have students compare their answers with a partner.

4. Go over the answers with the class.

Activity B Answers, p. 35
1. foreign language
2. campus
3. community
4. professor
5. active
6. skill

PREVIEW THE LISTENING

A (10 minutes)

1. Direct students to look at the picture. Ask: *What do you see? Where are these buildings? Do we have a campus like this?*

2. Read the sentences in Preview the Listening aloud. Have students match the places on the campus to their descriptions.

3. Go over the answers with the class.

4. Tell students they should review their answers after listening.

Activity A Answers, p. 35
1. c
2. a
3. b
4. d

B (5 minutes)

1. Go over the directions.

2. Put students in pairs to answer the questions.

3. Go over the answers with the class.

Activity B Answers, p. 35
Answers will vary. Possible answers: snack bar, bookstore, gym, auditorium, classrooms

Listening Background Note

At colleges and universities in English-speaking countries, the dining commons may also be called a dining hall or a cafeteria. Even at small colleges there may be more than one place to eat. Most schools offer special menus for students who are vegetarian or follow another specific diet.

Almost every university in the world offers Internet access to its students. Some universities only have it available in the library or computer labs, but at many students have connections in their dorms or wireless connections anywhere on campus.

▶ *Listening and Speaking Intro, page 36*

Comprehension Check

🔊 CD1, Track 22

A (10 minutes)

1. Go over the directions. Have students read the statements.
2. Play the audio and have students complete the activity individually.
3. Have students compare their answers with a partner.
4. Go over the answers with the class. For greater practice, play the audio again and have students correct the false statements.

> **Activity A Answers, p. 36**
> **1.** F; There is free Internet access in the library.
> **2.** F; All of the students live on campus.
> **3.** T
> **4.** F; The professors want students to talk.
> **5.** T
> **6.** T

Skill Review: Listening for examples
(5 minutes)

1. Read the skill review information aloud.
2. Remind students to listen for *like* and *for example* and then notice the information that follows.

B (10 minutes)
🔊 CD1, Track 22

1. Go over the directions. Have students read the sentences.
2. Play the audio and have students complete the activity individually.
3. Have students compare their answers with a partner.
4. Go over the answers with the class.

> **Activity B Answers, p. 36**
> **1.** a; **2.** c; **3.** c; **4.** d; **5.** b

EXPANSION ACTIVITY: Plan a Tour (15 minutes)

1. Explain the activity. Students will work in pairs to plan a tour of their school. They will draw a map and decide where the tour will begin and end, and what places will be on the tour. Then they will write a sentence about each place.
2. Have students work in pairs to draw their maps and plan the tour.
3. Have students write one sentence about each place on their tour.
4. Call on pairs of students to present their ideas to the class.

▶ *Listening and Speaking Intro, page 37*

Building Vocabulary: Using the dictionary: antonyms (5 minutes)

1. Direct students to read the information silently.
2. Go over the dictionary entry for *hard*. Point out that this word has two antonyms, depending on the context of the sentence.
3. Check comprehension by asking: *What is an antonym? Is its meaning the same or the opposite? What is the antonym of* good? *What is the antonym of* hard? *What is the antonym of* up?

Skill Note

Students may not recall what the different parts of speech are. If helpful, give an example of each part of speech and its antonym:

noun: man/woman

verb: give/take

adjective: tall/short

adverb: quickly/slowly

Tip for Success (1 minute)

1. Read the tip aloud.
2. Suggest students write any pairs of antonyms that are new to them in their vocabulary notebooks.
3. For more practice, have students work in pairs to list five pairs of antonyms they already know. Set a time limit of two minutes. Elicit ideas.

A (5 minutes)

1. Go over the directions. Say each word in the box and have students repeat.

2. Direct students to complete the activity individually.

3. Have students compare their answers with a partner.

4. Go over the answers with the class.

> **Activity A Answers, p. 37**
> **1.** easy
> **2.** succeed
> **3.** above
> **4.** strength
> **5.** negative
> **6.** complicated
> **7.** cheap
> **8.** badly

MULTILEVEL OPTION

Group lower-level students and assist them with the task. For each item, have students look up the word in the dictionary and confirm the answer as a group. Have higher-level students complete the activity on their own, then check their answers with their dictionaries. Have them choose four of the words to use in sentences.

B (10 minutes)

1. Go over the directions.

2. Have students complete the activity individually.

3. Have students compare their answers with a partner.

4. Go over the answers with the class. For more practice, call on students to read the sentences aloud.

> **Activity B Answers, pp. 37–38**
> **1.** dirty
> **2.** interesting
> **3.** weakness
> **4.** dangerous
> **5.** expensive
> **6.** succeed
> **7.** on
> **8.** easy

MULTILEVEL OPTION

Have higher-level students write sentences using the other word in each pair (the antonym not chosen). Call on volunteers to write sentences on the board. Suggest lower-level students copy the sentences in their notebooks.

▶ *Listening and Speaking Intro, page 38*

C (5 minutes)

1. Go over the directions and the examples.

2. Direct students to complete the activity individually.

3. Have students share their sentences in pairs.

4. Call on students to read their sentences to the class. Or have volunteers write sentences on the board.

> **Activity C Answers, p. 38**
> Answers will vary. Possible answers:
> clean: The dormitory is clean. The street is dirty.
> safe: My town is safe. That town is dangerous.
> interesting: This book is interesting. The movie is boring.

 For additional practice with using the dictionary, have students visit *Q Online Practice*.

WHAT DO YOU THINK?

A (10 minutes)

1. Go over the directions and the sentences.

2. Have students complete the activity individually.

> **Activity A Answers, p. 38**
> Answers will vary. Most if not all of the answers may be affirmative.

Critical Thinking Tip (1 minute)

1. Read the tip aloud.

2. Point out that people use their own ideas and knowledge when they discuss topics. Have students support each answer in Activity A with a reason.

Critical Q: Expansion Activity

Evaluation

1. Have a group of several students stand. Read the first statement. Give students a minute to silently consider their answers to the question. Then ask students who think the statement is very important to stand on one side of the room and students who think it is not important to stand on the other side of the room.
2. Direct students to tell a partner next to them their reasons for choosing that side of the issue.
3. Call on volunteers from each side to share their opinions with the class.
4. After students have shared their opinions, provide an opportunity for anyone who would like to change sides to do so.
5. Continue with other groups of students and other statements. Make sure everyone has a chance to explain his or her opinion on one of the statements.

B (10 minutes)

1. Go over the directions and the example.
2. Have students work in pairs to share their ideas.
3. Call on each pair or group to share their answers with the class.

> **Activity B Answers, p. 38**
> Answers will vary.

Learning Outcome

Use the Learning Outcome to frame the purpose and relevance of the Listening. Say: *The Learning Outcome is to share your opinions to plan a perfect school. What did you learn from the Listening? How will it help you plan a perfect school and present your ideas?*

(Students learned about places on a campus, and they discussed different features of a school.)

SPEAKING

Grammar: Adjectives; adverbs + adjectives (10 minutes)

1. Read the information about using adjectives and adverbs + adjectives. Provide and elicit additional examples: *She's (very) smart. He's a good soccer player. Our school has a (really) pretty campus. The campus is (really) pretty.*
2. Check comprehension by asking questions: *Is it OK to put an adjective before a noun? Does an adjective sometimes come after* be? *Do we usually put adjectives before verbs? Do adverbs change the meaning of the adjective a little?*

Skill Note

In this section, students are learning about adverbs that can strengthen the adjective, but adverbs can also weaken an adjective: *The class is somewhat interesting.* The point to focus on is that adverbs tell us more about the adjective. Remind students that adverbs can also describe verbs: *She works well with other people.*

▶ *Listening and Speaking Intro, page 40*

A (10 minutes)

1. Direct students' attention to the first sentence of the email. Have students tell you why *university new* is wrong. (Adjectives go before nouns.)
2. Direct students to complete the activity individually.
3. Have students compare their answers in pairs.
4. Go over the answers with the class.

> **Activity A Answers, p. 40**
> Well, I am now at my <u>new university</u>. It's in a <u>very large</u> city. It's pretty different from our small town. It's an extremely noisy <u>place</u>, but I love it. There are <u>excellent</u> museums and parks, and the weather is perfect. The school doesn't have dormitories. I live in an <u>expensive apartment</u> in the city. The apartment building is <u>really beautiful</u>, but it's pretty old. I have a really great roommate. His name is Joe. My school is great, but my classes are <u>extremely big</u>. Some of my classes have 200 people in them! However, my professors are <u>very good</u> and my classes are really interesting. We have a <u>great science</u> laboratory. I study biology there. I'm learning a lot. Also, the people here are <u>very friendly</u>, but I miss my old friends.

B (10 minutes)

1. Go over the directions.
2. Direct students to complete the activity individually.
3. Have students compare their answers in pairs.
4. Elicit ideas from the class.
5. Have students practice the conversation in pairs.

> **Activity B Answers, p. 40**
> Answers will vary. Possible answers: very good; great, interesting; really big; pretty nice

 For additional practice with adjectives and adverbs + adjectives, have students visit *Q Online Practice*.

▶ *Listening and Speaking Intro, page 41*
Pronunciation: Sentence stress (5 minutes)

CD1, Track 23

1. Read the information about sentence stress.
2. Play the audio.
3. Check comprehension by asking questions: *What do we do when we stress words? What words are usually stressed? Do we usually stress the verb* be? *Do we usually stress articles? What other words are not stressed?*

A (15 minutes)

CD1, Track 24

1. Go over the directions.
2. Direct students to complete the activity individually.
3. Play the audio so students can check their answers.
4. Go over the answers with the class.
5. Have students work in pairs to practice saying the sentences.

> **Activity A Answers, p. 41**
> 1. school, lacrosse, team
> 2. two, classes, morning
> 3. want, safe, clean, school
> 4. college, dangerous, city
> 5. coffee shops, free, Internet, access
> 6. What, good, school
> 7. sports, field, pretty, big
> 8. school, really, great
> 9. buses, school, very, slow
> 10. When, class, begin

B (5–10 minutes)

1. Go over the directions.
2. Direct students to complete the activity individually.
3. Call on students and elicit a few examples.

> **Activity B Answers, p. 41**
> Answers will vary. Possible answers:
> My school is pretty small.
> The library is really big.
> The dormitory is very clean.
> The sports field is extremely large.
> The professors are really good.

C (5–10 minutes)

1. Go over the directions.
2. Have students exchange papers with a partner.
3. Direct students to underline the stressed words on their partner's paper.
4. Have students practice reading the sentences aloud.
5. Have volunteers write sentences on the board. Ask the class to identify the stressed words. Practice saying the sentences as a class.

> **Activity C Answers, p. 41**
> Answers will vary.

 For additional practice with sentence stress, have students visit *Q Online Practice*.

▶ *Listening and Speaking Intro, page 42*
Speaking Skill: Giving opinions (5 minutes)

CD1, Track 25

1. Read the information about giving opinions.
2. Play the audio.
3. Check comprehension by asking: *What words do we use to give opinions? What words mean your opinion is the same? What words mean your opinion is different?*

Tip for Success (1 minute)

1. Read the tip aloud.
2. Point out that students can use the punctuation in Activity A to help them confirm their answers.
3. Suggest students pay attention to the use of commas when they are learning other expressions in later units.

A (10 minutes)

CD1, Track 26

1. Go over the directions.
2. Play the audio and have students complete the conversations.
3. Have students compare their answers with a partner.
4. Go over the answers with the class.
5. Have students practice the conversations in pairs.

> **Activity A Answers, p. 42**
> **1.** In my opinion; I disagree
> **2.** I think that; I agree
> **3.** In my opinion; I agree; I think that
> **4.** In my opinion; I disagree; I think that
> **5.** I think that; I disagree; In my opinion

▶ *Listening and Speaking Intro, page 43*

B (10 minutes)

1. Go over the directions.
2. Have students write answers to the questions.
3. Have students take turns asking and answering the questions in pairs.
4. Call on students and ask the questions. Remind students to begin with *I think that* or *In my opinion.*

> **Activity B Answers, p. 43**
> Answers will vary. Possible answers:
> **1.** I think that 15 is the perfect number of students in a foreign language class.
> **2.** In my opinion, good discussions and activities make a class interesting.
> **3.** I think that it's better to work in a group because students can help each other.

 For additional practice with giving opinions, have students visit *Q Online Practice.*

Q Unit Assignment: Plan a perfect school

Unit Question (5 minutes)

Refer students back to the ideas they discussed at the beginning of the unit about what makes a good school. Cue students if necessary by asking specific questions about the content of the unit: *What kind of campus does a good school have? How big are the classes? What makes a class good?*

Learning Outcome

1. Tie the Unit Assignment to the unit Learning Outcome. Say: *The outcome for this unit is to share your opinions to plan a perfect school and present your ideas to the class. This Unit Assignment is going to let you show your skill in planning a perfect school with others and in presenting your ideas to the class.*
2. Explain that you are going to use a rubric similar to their Self-Assessment checklist on p. 44 to grade their Unit Assignment. You can also share a copy of the Unit Assignment Rubric (on p. 28 of this *Teacher's Handbook*) with the students.

Consider the Ideas (10 minutes)

CD1, Track 27

1. Go over the directions and the sentences.
2. Play the audio and direct students to check the boxes.
3. Have students compare their answers with a partner.
4. Go over the answers with the class.

> **Consider the Ideas Answers, p. 44**
> Check 1, 2, 4, 5, 7

21ST CENTURY SKILLS

Flexibility and the willingness to help others to achieve a common goal are important qualities on academic and professional teams. Whether students are making a group presentation to their class, to their customers, or to a professional organization, they have to be willing to change their ideas or roles so that each member can do his or her best. Encourage groups to come up with a plan for the presentation that ensures everyone feels comfortable with the topic and can participate fully.

Prepare and Speak

Gather Ideas

Tip for Success (1 minute)

1. Read the tip aloud.

2. Encourage students to give examples and add information as they work in their groups.

A (10 minutes)

1. Go over the directions and the questions or have students read them silently.

2. Have students work individually to write answers in their notebooks.

3. Direct students to share their ideas, using *I think that* and *In my opinion.*

4. Call on students to share their ideas with the class.

Organize Ideas

B (20 minutes)

1. Go over the directions.

2. Have students work in the same small groups to follow the steps.

3. Walk around the room and provide help as needed.

Speak

C (30 minutes)

1. Go over the directions.

2. Have students review the Self-Assessment checklist on p. 44 to note what they should include in their presentation. Suggest they review the vocabulary on p. 34 and the information on adjectives and adverb + adjective combinations on p. 39 if helpful.

3. Use the Unit Assignment Rubric on p. 28 of this *Teacher's Handbook* to score each student's presentation.

4. Alternatively, have each group join another group and have these groups present their plans to each other. Have listeners complete the Unit Assignment Rubric.

Check and Reflect

Check

A (5 minutes)

1. Direct students to read and complete the Self-Assessment checklist.

2. Ask for a show of hands for how many students gave all or mostly *yes* answers.

3. Congratulate them on their success. Discuss the steps they can take if an item on the checklist was difficult for them. For example, they can review that section of the unit and plan to practice it over the next week.

Listening and Speaking Intro, page 45

Reflect

B (5 minutes)

1. Direct students to discuss the questions with a partner.

2. Elicit ideas from the class.

3. Ask students if the unit prepared them to plan a perfect school and present their plan to the class.

Track Your Success

1. Have students circle the words they have learned in this unit. Suggest that students go back through the unit to review any words they have forgotten.

2. Have students check the skills they have mastered. If students need more practice to feel confident about their proficiency in a skill, point out the page numbers and encourage them to review.

3. Read the Learning Outcome aloud. Ask students if they feel that they have met the outcome.

Unit Assignment Rubric

Student name: _____

Date: _____

Unit Assignment: *Plan a perfect school.*

20 points = Presentation element was completely successful (at least 90% of the time).
15 points = Presentation element was mostly successful (at least 70% of the time).
10 points = Presentation element was partially successful (at least 50% of the time).
 0 points = Presentation element was not successful.

Present a plan to the class	20 points	15 points	10 points	0 points
Student gave his/her opinion clearly.				
Student used vocabulary from the unit.				
Student used adjectives and adverbs + adjectives correctly.				
Students included at least one example of detail to support his/her opinion.				
Student used sentence stress correctly.				

Total points: _____

Comments:

4

Unit QUESTION

How do you choose your food?

Food

LISTENING • listening for reasons
VOCABULARY • prefixes and suffixes
GRAMMAR • verbs + gerunds or infinitives
PRONUNCIATION • stressed syllables
SPEAKING • giving opinions

LEARNING OUTCOME

Develop and tell a story about a personal experience using information on what makes a good story

▶ *Listening and Speaking Intro, page 47*

Preview the Unit

Learning Outcome

1. Ask for a volunteer to read the unit skills and then the unit Learning Outcome.

2. Explain: *Your goal for the unit is to be able to interview a classmate about his or her food preferences. I will use this Learning Outcome to grade your work at the end of the unit. Focus on learning these skills: Listening, Vocabulary, Grammar, Pronunciation, Speaking. They will help you reach your goal.*

A (10 minutes)

1. Say each word in the box and have students repeat.

2. Have students cross out the adjectives individually and then compare answers in pairs. Point out that some food is safer and healthier than other food, but we don't describe food as *dangerous*.

3. Call on volunteers to share their ideas with the class. Ask questions: *Who likes spicy food? What is something sweet? What is your favorite salty food? Which foods are good for you?*

> **Activity A Answers, p. 47**
> Crossed out: active, close, important, difficult

MULTILEVEL OPTION

Group lower-level students to go over the vocabulary in the box. Allow students to use a dictionary for unfamiliar words. Have higher-level students work in pairs to write sentences for three of the words in the box. Call on students to share their ideas with the class.

B (5 minutes)

1. Focus students' attention on the photo. Have a volunteer describe the photo to the class. Read the question aloud. Elicit answers.

2. Ask additional questions: *Do you have places like this near you? What do you like to eat at places like this?*

> **Activity B Answers, p. 47**
> Answers will vary. Possible answers: Eating. People are buying and serving food. People are buying and serving food in a food court or market.

C (10 minutes)

1. Introduce the Unit Question: "How do you choose your food?" Ask related information questions or questions about personal experience. Ask: *Is taste important? Do you care about your health?* Remind students to draw on their answers from Activities A and B.

2. Label four pieces of poster paper *(Taste, Price, Health, and Other)* and place them in the corners of the room. Make sure students understand what the labels mean.

3. Ask students to read and consider the Unit Question for a moment and then to stand in the corner next to the poster that best represents their answer to the question.

4. Direct the groups in each corner to talk among themselves about the reasons for their answer. Tell them to choose a secretary to record the answers on the poster paper.

5. Call on volunteers from each corner to share their opinions with the class.

6. Leave the posters up for students to refer back to at the end of the unit.

Answers will vary. Possible answers: Health. Healthy food. I choose healthy food.
I like salty/sweet/sour food. I like Chinese food. I like a lot of vegetables/meat/fruit.

The Q Classroom
CD1, Track 28

1. Play *The Q Classroom*. Use the example from the audio to help students continue the conversation. Ask: *What did the students say? What foods do they like? Which student likes spicy food? Who doesn't eat sugar?*

2. Ask additional questions: *Do you eat spicy food? Why or why not? Is fast food healthy? What foods do you like?*

▶ *Listening and Speaking Intro, page 48*

LISTENING

LISTENING: Lifestyles and Food Choices

VOCABULARY

A (10 minutes)

1. Go over the meaning of the word *ingredients*. Go over the definitions in the box.

2. Read the first sentence and elicit the word *(artificial)*. Have students write *artificial* on the line.

3. Direct students to complete the activity individually.

4. Have students compare their answers with a partner.

5. Go over the answers with the class.

MULTILEVEL OPTION

Group lower-level students and assist them with the task. Provide example sentences to help them understand the words. For example: *I am not good at math, so I **avoid** math classes./My apartment building has **artificial** plants in the lobby. They aren't real./The bus stop is very **convenient**. It's right in front of my building./I like **organic** food. It doesn't have chemicals.* Have higher-level students complete the activity individually and then compare answers with a partner. Tell the pairs to write an additional sample sentence for each word. Have volunteers write one of their sentences on the board. Correct the sentences with the whole class, focusing on the use of the expression rather than on other grammatical issues.

Activity A Answers, p. 48
1. artificial
2. nutritious
3. social
4. avoid
5. flavor
6. vegetarian
7. organic
8. convenient

▶ *Listening and Speaking Intro, page 49*

B (10 minutes)

1. Ask the first question and elicit answers.

2. Direct students to complete the activity individually.

3. Have students compare their answers with a partner.

4. Go over the answers with the class.

5. Have students take turns asking and answering the questions in pairs.

Tip for Success (1 minute)

1. Read the tip aloud.

2. Give examples: *Everyone needs food to live. Some of my favorite foods are bananas and cereal.*

3. If helpful, provide or elicit examples of other count nouns *(apples, bananas, cookies)* and noncount nouns *(milk, sugar, cheese)*.

Activity B Answers, p. 49
Answers will vary. Possible answers:
1. a sandwich
2. a pepper
3. I eat meat.
4. I don't eat it very often.
5. Yes, I do. I think artificial ingredients are bad for you.
6. apples, broccoli, spinach

PREVIEW THE LISTENING (5 minutes)

1. Direct students' attention to the picture. Ask: *Who do you see? Where are they?*

2. Read the questions aloud.

3. Have students complete the activity individually.

4. Have students compare their answers with a partner.

5. Elicit ideas from the class.

Preview the Listening Answers, p. 49
Answers will vary.

Listening Background Note

One of the speakers is vegetarian, meaning he does not eat animals, although some vegetarians eat eggs and dairy products. The popularity of vegetarianism varies around the world. About 30 percent of the population in India is vegetarian, 6 percent in the United Kingdom, and 3-4 percent in the United States. Vegetarianism is quite rare in some places, like South America.

In general, organic food is grown without chemicals. Farmers don't use pesticides on their fruits and vegetables, and they don't give their animals hormones and antibiotics.

▶ *Listening and Speaking Intro, page 50*

Comprehension Check

 CD1, Track 29

A (10 minutes)

1. Have students read the information.
2. Play the audio and have students complete the activity individually.
3. Have students compare their answers with a partner.
4. Go over the answers with the class.

> **Activity A Answers, p. 50**
> **1.** c
> **2.** a
> **3.** b
> **4.** d

B (15 minutes)

1. Have students read the information.
2. Play the audio again and have students complete the activity individually.
3. Have students compare their answers with a partner. If necessary, play the audio one more time.
4. Go over the answers with the class.

> **Activity B Answers, p. 50**
> **1.** a, b, d
> **2.** c, f
> **3.** g, i, j
> **4.** e, h

EXPANSION ACTIVITY: (10 minutes)

1. Explain the activity. Students will prepare to talk for 30-60 seconds about their own reasons for food choices.
2. Have students work individually to check the items (a-j) that are true for them. Direct them to add one more item.
3. Have students review the items that describe them.
4. Put students in groups of three or four to take turns talking about their own food habits and choices. Encourage students to speak without looking at their books.
5. Call on volunteers to share their ideas with the class.

▶ *Listening and Speaking Intro, page 51*

Building Vocabulary: Prefixes and suffixes (5 minutes)

1. Direct students to read the information silently.
2. Check comprehension of the information and the dictionary entries: *What prefixes mean* not? *What suffix means* not? *What word means a food has no salt? A food has no fat? A situation that isn't safe? What is the meaning of* nonstop flight?

Skill Note

Prefixes usually change the meaning of a word (*happy* and *unhappy* are antonyms), whereas suffixes usually change the part of speech (*happy* is an adjective, *happiness* is a noun). Although the prefixes and suffixes in this lesson have similar meanings, they follow these rules. *Non-* and *un-* change the meaning of words that are used as adjectives. The suffix *-free* changes a noun to an adjective. A noun + *free* is usually hyphenated.

A (5 minutes)

1. Read the first item aloud. Elicit the completion (*nonfat*).
2. Direct students to complete the activity individually.
3. Have students compare their answers with a partner.
4. Go over the answers with the class.

Activity A Answers, pp. 51–52
1. nonfat
2. unhealthy
3. unfriendly
4. nondairy
5. salt-free
6. unsafe
7. sugar-free
8. unusual

MULTILEVEL OPTION

Group lower-level students. Have them discuss or look up definitions for each word in the box. Then have students identify words in each sentence that can help them choose the correct word (1. fat; 2. junk food, sick; 3. doesn't talk to anyone; 4. milk, cheese, butter; 5. salt; 6. artificial; 7. avoid, sugar; 8. same). Have higher-level students write alternate sentences for each word.

▶ *Listening and Speaking Intro, page 52*

B (10 minutes)

1. Model the activity. Tell the class about one sentence that is true for you.
2. Have students complete the activity individually.
3. Have students compare their answers with a partner.
4. Call on students to tell the class a statement that is true for them.

Activity B Answers, p. 52
Answers will vary.

C (5 minutes)

1. Go over the directions.
2. Direct students to complete the activity individually.
3. Have students share their sentences in pairs.
4. Call on students to read their sentences to the class. Or have volunteers write sentences on the board.

Activity C Answers, p. 52
Answers will vary. Possible answers:
nonviolent: I only play nonviolent video games.
carefree: I'm usually happy and carefree.
unfriendly: I don't like unfriendly people.

 For additional practice with prefixes and suffixes, have students visit *Q Online Practice*.

Pronunciation: Stressed syllables
(5 minutes)

🔊 CD1 Track 30

1. Read the information about sentence stress.
2. Play the audio.
3. Check comprehension by asking questions: *What syllable is stressed in* organic? *What syllable is stressed in* vegetarian?

A (10 minutes)
🔊 CD1 Track 31

1. Direct students to complete the activity individually.
2. Play the audio.
3. Go over the answers with the class.
4. Have students work in pairs to practice saying the words

Activity A Answers, p. 52
1. de**li**cious
2. al**ler**gic
3. un**health**y
4. edu**ca**tion
5. con**ven**tion
6. **su**gar-**free**
7. **gar**den
8. **din**ner
9. **dai**ry
10. com**mu**nity

MULTILEVEL OPTION

As lower-level students work in pairs to practice saying the words, have higher-level students write sentences for each word and practice saying them in pairs.

▶ *Listening and Speaking Intro, page 53*

B (5-10 minutes)
🔊 CD1, Track 32

1. Play the audio and direct students to circle the stressed syllables.
2. Have students compare their answers with a partner.

Activity B Answers, p. 53
1. In my o<u>pin</u>ion, arti<u>fi</u>cial in<u>gre</u>dients are un<u>safe</u>.
2. He <u>doesn't</u> eat <u>chick</u>en or beef.
3. He wants to lose weight, so he's on a <u>diet</u>.
4. This soup has an un<u>usual flavor</u>.
5. Are these <u>cookies</u> sugar-<u>free</u>?
6. She grows or<u>gan</u>ic to<u>ma</u>toes in her <u>garden</u>.

Tip for Success (1 minute)

1. Read the tip aloud.
2. Have students read the sentences in Activity B to notice the pronouns, prepositions, and articles.

C (5 minutes)

 CD1, Track 33

1. Play the audio again and have students underline the stressed words.
2. Go over the answers with the class.

> **Activity C Answers, p. 53**
> **1.** In my <u>opinion</u>, <u>artificial</u> <u>ingredients</u> are <u>unsafe</u>.
> **2.** He <u>doesn't</u> eat <u>chicken</u> or <u>beef</u>.
> **3.** He <u>wants</u> to <u>lose</u> <u>weight</u>, so he's on a <u>diet</u>.
> **4.** This <u>soup</u> has an <u>unusual</u> <u>flavor</u>.
> **5.** Are these <u>cookies</u> <u>sugar-free</u>?
> **6.** She <u>grows</u> <u>organic</u> <u>tomatoes</u> in her <u>garden</u>.

 For additional practice with stressed syllables, have students visit *Q Online Practice*.

Listening Skill: Listening for reasons
(5 minutes)

 CD1, Track 34

1. Play the audio and have students read along silently.
2. Check comprehension by asking questions: *What question word asks for reasons? What word do we use to give reasons?*

A (10 minutes)
 CD1, Track 35

1. Direct students' attention to the picture in the margin.
2. Direct students to read the questions and possible answers.
3. Play the audio and have students complete the activity individually.
4. Have students compare their answers in pairs. If necessary, play the audio again.
5. Go over the answers with the class.
6. Have students read the questions and answers in pairs.

> **Activity A Answers, pp. 53–54**
> **1.** c   **2.** b   **3.** b   **4.** a

 Listening and Speaking Intro, page 54

B (5 minutes)

1. Model the activity. Tell students which of the four people you are similar to and why.
2. Have students share their ideas in pairs.
3. Go over the answers with the class.

> **Activity B Answers, p. 54**
> Answers will vary.

 For additional practice with listening for reasons, have students visit *Q Online Practice*.

WHAT DO YOU THINK?

A (5 minutes)

1. Go over the questions.
2. Have students complete the activity individually.

> **Activity A Answers, p. 54**
> Answers will vary.

B (5 minutes)

1. Go over the directions and the examples.
2. Have students work in pairs to share their ideas.
3. Call on each pair or group to share their answers with the class.

> **Activity B Answers, p. 54**
> Answers will vary.

Tip for Success (1 minute)

1 Read the tip aloud.
2. If helpful, provide more examples: *Why do you eat vegetables? Why don't you eat organic food?*

Learning Outcome

Use the Learning Outcome to frame the purpose and relevance of the Listening. Say: *The Learning Outcome is to design a survey about food and interview a classmate about his or her food choices. What did you learn from the Listening? How will it help you interview a classmate?*

(Students learned about different reasons for food choices.)

SPEAKING

Grammar: Verbs + gerunds or infinitives (10 minutes)

1. Read the information about using verbs + gerunds or infinitives. Provide and elicit additional examples: *He enjoys playing video games. I want to see a movie. She likes to dance/dancing.*

2. Explain that the phrase *can't stand* means "hate" or "really dislike" (something).

3. Check comprehension by asking questions: *What form follows* enjoy? *Is it OK to say* I need buying groceries? *What form follows the verb* love?

Skill Note

Students sometimes get confused about the difference between the progressive (continuous) form of the verb (e.g., *We are eating dinner now*) and the gerund. Help students to focus on using these verbs as part of expressions or collocations, rather than on the terminology. The infinitives and gerunds are objects of the verbs here, so it might help students to think of them as activities.

▶ *Listening and Speaking Intro, page 56*

A (10 minutes)

🔊 CD1, Track 36

1. Play the audio. Stop after the first sentence and point out that *to cook* is circled.

2. Continue to play the audio and have students complete the activity individually.

3. Have students compare their answers in pairs. Play the audio again if necessary.

4. Go over the answers with the class.

> **Activity A Answers, p. 56**
> **2.** to eat   **3.** shopping
> **4.** buying   **5.** to eat
> **6.** to avoid   **7.** cooking
> **8.** eating   **9.** to eat
> **10.** going

B (10 minutes)

1. Model the activity. Read the first few sentences aloud. Elicit the completion for item 1 *(to cook/cooking)*. Remind students that in some sentences they can use either a gerund or an infinitive.

2. Direct students to complete the activity individually.

3. Have students compare their answers in pairs.

4. Go over the answers with the class.

5. Have students practice the conversation in pairs.

> **Activity B Answers, p. 56**
> **1.** to cook/cooking
> **2.** to eat/eating
> **3.** trying
> **4.** eating
> **5.** to avoid
> **6.** to cook
> **7.** to start

▶ *Listening and Speaking Intro, page 57*

C (15 minutes)

1. Model the activity. Complete the first sentence about you, e.g., *I want to bake a cake.*

2. Direct students to complete the activity individually.

3. Have students compare their ideas in pairs.

4. Elicit sentences from the class.

> **Activity C Answers, p. 57**
> Answers will vary. Possible answers:
> **1.** I want to find a new restaurant.
> **2.** I need to cook dinner tonight.
> **3.** I avoid eating sugar.
> **4.** I try to drink a lot of water.
> **5.** I like to go food shopping.
> **6.** I love to have dessert.
> **7.** I hate feeling too full.
> **8.** I enjoy baking bread.

For additional practice with verbs + gerunds or infinitives, have students visit *Q Online Practice.*

Unit Assignment: Design a survey and interview a classmate

Unit Question (5 minutes)

Refer students back to the ideas they discussed at the beginning of the unit about how they choose food. Cue students if necessary by asking specific questions about the content of the unit: *What is important to you about food? Do you eat unhealthy food? Do you eat nonfat foods? Do you prefer organic food?*

Learning Outcome

1. Tie the Unit Assignment to the unit Learning Outcome. Say: *The outcome for this unit is to design a survey about food and interview a classmate about food choices. This Unit Assignment is going to let you show your skill in asking and answering questions about food.*

2. Explain that you are going to use a rubric similar to their Self-Assessment checklist on p. 58 to grade their Unit Assignment. You can also share a copy of the Unit Assignment Rubric (on p. 37 of this *Teacher's Handbook*) with the students.

Consider the Ideas (15 minutes)

🔊 CD1, Track 37

1. Play the audio and direct students to match the questions and answers.

2. Have students compare their answers with a partner.

3. Go over the answers with the class.

> **Consider the Ideas Answers, p. 57**
> **1.** e
> **2.** c
> **3.** a
> **4.** b
> **5.** d

▶ *Listening and Speaking Intro, page 58*

Prepare and Speak

Gather Ideas

A (10 minutes)

1. Go over the directions.

2. Have students work in pairs to write ten questions in their notebooks.

3. Call on students to share their ideas with the class.

Organize Ideas

B (5 minutes)

1. Have students work in the same pairs to follow the steps.

2. Walk around the room and provide help as needed.

Skill Review: Giving opinions (3 minutes)

1. Have students read the information in the box. If they need more review, refer them to p. 42.

2. Suggest interviewers make a checkmark next to each answer that begins with the phrases *In my opinion* or *I think that.*

Speak

Tip for Success (1 minute)

1. Read the tip aloud.

2. Encourage students to add one follow-up question to each question on their survey.

C (10 minutes)

1. Go over the directions.

2. Have students review the Self-Assessment checklist on p. 58 to note what they should include in their interview. Suggest they review the vocabulary on p. 48 and the information on gerunds and infinitives on p. 55 if helpful.

3. Use the Unit Assignment Rubric on p. 37 of this *Teacher's Handbook* to score each student's interview. Have each partner complete the assessment for the other.

4. Alternatively, have each pair join another pair. Have pairs conduct their interviews in front of each other. Have the original partners complete the Unit Assignment Rubric.

21ST CENTURY SKILLS

Being able to respond to questions thoughtfully and appropriately is an important skill in any academic or professional setting. Phrases that signal an opinion can soften a response, making it easier to carry on a productive discussion. To provide even more practice with these expressions call on students to pose one of their interview questions to a different classmate. Make sure the student responds with *In my opinion* or *I think that.*

Critical Thinking Tip (1 minute)

1. Read the critical thinking tip aloud.

2. Point out that when we summarize, we tell only the main ideas, and we often combine information.

Critical Q: Expansion Activity

Summarizing

1. Say: *When you summarize, you give the important information but in a shorter form.*

2. To help students practice summarizing, suggest they take notes as they listen to students talk about their interview results.

3. Have students write sentences summarizing what they hear, e.g., *Most students like healthy food. Many students eat meat.*

4. Have students compare sentences in pairs or small groups.

5. Call on students to share their ideas with the class.

Check and Reflect

Check

A (5 minutes)

1. Direct students to read and complete the Self-Assessment checklist.

2. Ask for a show of hands for how many students gave all or mostly *yes* answers.

3. Congratulate them on their success. Discuss the steps they can take if an item on the checklist was difficult for them. For example, if students had difficulty with gerunds and infinitives, suggest they write down examples they see and hear over the next week.

▶ *Listening and Speaking Intro, page 59*

Reflect

B (5 minutes)

1. Direct students to discuss the questions with a partner.

2. Elicit ideas from the class.

3. Ask students if the unit prepared them to interview a classmate about food choices.

Track Your Success

1. Have students circle the words they have learned in this unit. Suggest that students go back through the unit to review any words they have forgotten.

2. Have students check the skills they have mastered. If students need more practice to feel confident about their proficiency in a skill, point out the page numbers and encourage them to review.

3. Read the Learning Outcome aloud. Ask students if they feel that they have met the outcome.

Unit Assignment Rubric

Student name: _____

Date: _____

Unit Assignment: *Design a survey and interview a classmate.*

20 points = Interview element was completely successful (at least 90% of the time).
15 points = Interview element was mostly successful (at least 70% of the time).
10 points = Interview element was partially successful (at least 50% of the time).
 0 points = Interview element was not successful.

Interview a classmate	20 points	15 points	10 points	0 points
Student's interview questions were clear.				
Students asked follow-up questions.				
Student used vocabulary from the unit.				
Student used gerunds and infinitives correctly.				
Student gave reasons for opinions when answering questions.				

Total points: _____

Comments:

Unit QUESTION

What makes something fun?

Fun

LISTENING • listening for reasons
VOCABULARY • collocations with *do, play,* and *go*
GRAMMAR • subject and object pronouns
PRONUNCIATION • reduced pronouns
SPEAKING • agreeing and disagreeing

LEARNING OUTCOME

Participate in a group discussion about fun places in your area.

▶ *Listening and Speaking Intro, page 61*

Preview the Unit

Learning Outcome

1. Ask for a volunteer to read the unit skills and then the unit Learning Outcome.

2. Explain: *Your goal for the unit is to be able to participate in a group discussion about fun places in your area. I will use this Learning Outcome to grade your work at the end of the unit. Focus on learning these skills: Listening, Vocabulary, Grammar, Pronunciation, Speaking. They will help you reach your goal.*

A (10 minutes)

1. Have students complete the chart individually and then compare their ideas with a partner.

2. Call on volunteers to share their ideas with the class. Ask questions: *Is playing soccer fun? Is homework boring? Who likes dangerous activities? What is something exciting?*

Activity A Answers, p. 61
Answers will vary. Possible answers:
a fun activity: the movies
a boring activity: video games
an exciting activity: a concert
a dangerous activity: skiing
an interesting activity: hiking

MULTILEVEL OPTION

Group lower-level students to brainstorm vocabulary for activities. Have higher-level students work in pairs to add two more activities to each description in the chart. Call on students to share their ideas with the class.

B (5 minutes)

1. Focus students' attention on the photo. Have a volunteer describe the photo to the class. Read the question aloud. Elicit answers.

2. Ask additional questions: *Why do people do this? Do you like to be in races? Do you like to do hard things?*

Activity B Answers, p. 61
Answers will vary. Possible answers:
A race/a competition. They are in a race. They are competing in a race.

C (10 minutes)

1. Introduce the Unit Question: "What makes something fun?" Ask related information questions or questions about personal experience: *Do you like to do things with friends? Is fun the same for everyone?* Remind students to draw on their answers from Activities A and B.

2. Read the Unit Question aloud. Point out that answers to the question can fall into categories. (*Who do you do it with? Where do you do it? How active is it? How often do you do it?*) Give students a minute to silently consider their answers to the question.

3. Write each category at the top of a sheet of poster paper. Elicit answers for the question and make notes of the answers under the correct heading. Post the lists to refer to later in the unit.

Activity C Answers, p. 61
Answers will vary. Possible answers:
Friends. Friends are fun. Friends make something fun.

The Q Classroom

 CD1, Track 38

1. Play *The Q Classroom*. Use the example from the audio to help students continue the conversation. Ask: *What did the students say? What are some things they like to do? Do they think the same things are fun that you do?*

2. Have students talk in pairs about which student from *The Q Classroom* they want to spend the day with.

▶ *Listening and Speaking Intro, page 62*

LISTENING

LISTENING: Why Do You Come to the Park?

VOCABULARY (10 minutes)

1. Go over the sentences.

2. Direct students to complete the activity individually.

3. Have students compare their answers with a partner.

4. Go over the answers with the class.

MULTILEVEL OPTION

Group lower-level students and assist them with the task. Provide alternate example sentences to help them understand the words. For example: *I don't like **modern** buildings. I like historical places./There's a bike **path** in my neighborhood. It's much safer than riding on the streets./My favorite vacation is at the beach. It's very **relaxing** to lie in the sun.*

Have higher-level students complete the activity individually and then compare their answers with a partner. Tell the pairs to write an additional sample sentence for each word. Have volunteers write one of their sentences on the board. Correct the sentences with the whole class, focusing on the use of the words rather than on other grammatical issues.

Vocabulary Answers, p. 63
1. relaxing
2. modern
3. crowded
4. path
5. nature
6. concert
7. outdoors
8. sculptures

▶ *Listening and Speaking Intro, page 63*

PREVIEW LISTENING (10 minutes)

1. Direct students' attention to the map. Ask questions: *What is the name of the park? What city is it in? What is one place you see on the map?*

2. Put students in pairs to answer the questions.

3. Go over the answers with the class.

Activity B Answers, p. 63
Answers will vary. Possible answers:
gardens, lake, paths, roads, sports fields

Listening Background Note

Ibirapuera Park is the second largest park in Saõ Paulo, Brazil. It opened in 1954 to celebrate the 400th birthday of the city. It houses several museums, a free library where people can borrow magazines and newspapers for the day, and an auditorium. Admission to the park is free.

▶ *Listening and Speaking Intro, page 64*

Skill Review: Listening for reasons (5 minutes)

1. Read the skill review information aloud.

2. Remind students to listen for *why* and *because* and then to notice the information that follows.

Comprehension Check

A (10 minutes)

 CD1, Track 39

1. Have students read the statements.

2. Play the audio and have students complete the activity individually.

3. Have students compare their answers with a partner.

4. Go over the answers with the class.

Activity A Answers, p. 64
1. a, c; **2.** d

B (10 minutes)

1. Have students read the questions and answers.

2. Play the audio and have students complete the activity individually.

3. Have students compare their answers with a partner.

4. Go over the answers with the class.

EXPANSION ACTIVITY: Isabel or Carlos? (10 minutes)

1. Model the activity. Tell students who you are more like: Isabel or Carlos. Then tell the class where you would take your new "friend," e.g., *I am going to take Isabel to the Museum of Modern Art downtown because we both like sculptures. Also, someone usually plays music in the lobby of the museum.*

2. Have students decide if they are more like Isabel or Carlos. Then have students work individually to plan a place they would go to with the person they are more like.

3. Have students share their plan with a partner.

4. Call on students to share their ideas with the class.

▶ *Listening and Speaking Intro, page 65–66*

Building Vocabulary: Collocations with *do, play,* and *go* (5 minutes)

1. Direct students to read the information silently.

2. Check comprehension: *What is an activity you do? What can you play? What kind of word usually follows* go?

Skill Note

Students sometimes think there is a shortcut to using collocations, but they really just need to learn and practice them. To encourage the memorization process have students review the expressions for two minutes. With books closed, call on students and say a verb, eliciting an appropriate completion. Then call on students and say an activity, eliciting the appropriate verb.

Tip for Success (1 minute)

1. Read the tip aloud.

2. Suggest students practice the collocations in pairs using *Let's:* e.g., *Let's do yoga. Let's play chess. Let's go shopping.*

A (5 minutes)

1. Read the first exchange between Sam and Emma. Elicit the completion for the first blank (*go*). Have students write *go* on the line.

2. Direct students to complete the activity individually.

3. Have students compare their answers with a partner.

4. Go over the answers with the class.

Activity A Answers, pp. 65-66
1. go; play; go
2. do; do
3. go; play; play; go

MULTILEVEL OPTION

Have lower-level students practice reading the conversations in pairs. Have higher-level students work in pairs to create alternate conversations. Ask volunteers to read their conversations to the class.

▶ *Listening and Speaking Intro, page 67*

B (10 minutes)

1. Model the activity. Tell the class what you like to do on weekends.

2. Have students complete the activity individually.

3. Have students compare their answers with a partner.

4. Elicit ideas from the class. Have students ask and answer the questions in pairs.

Activity B Answers, p. 67
Answers will vary. Possible answers:
1. I like to do nothing.
2. I like to play video games.
3. I like to go swimming.
4. I really hate to go jogging.

Critical Thinking Tip (1 minute)

1. Read the tip aloud.

2. Point out that practicing new skills and reviewing information every day helps students remember better.

3. Suggest students make a habit of practicing new vocabulary words by using them in sentences outside class.

Critical Q: Expansion Activity

Practice

1. Point out that practicing is the best way to move information from our short-term memory into our long-term memory.
2. Direct students to make notes about what other people in their families like to do at different times for fun. Lower-level students may want to actually write sentences. Remind students to use collocations with *do*, *play*, and *go*. For additional practice, suggest they use *like*, *don't like*, *love*, and *hate*.
3. Have students work in pairs to practice speaking for one minute about people they know and what they like to do for fun.
4. Call on students to speak to the class for one minute.

 For additional practice with collocations with *do*, *play*, and *go*, have students visit *Q Online Practice*.

WHAT DO YOU THINK?

A (10 minutes)

1. Go over the directions and the sentences.
2. Have students complete the activity individually.

> **Activity A Answers, p. 67**
> Answers will vary.

B (10 minutes)

1. Go over the questions.
2. Have students work in pairs to share their ideas.
3. Call on each pair or group to share their answers with the class.

> **Activity B Answers, p. 67**
> Answers will vary.

Learning Outcome

Use the Learning Outcome to frame the purpose and relevance of the Listening. Say: *The Learning Outcome is to participate in a group discussion about fun places in your area. What did you learn from the Listening? How will it help you to discuss fun places in a group?*

(Students learned about fun things people can do at a park. They also learned collocations with *do*, *play*, and *go* that they can use to talk about activities.)

▶ *Listening and Speaking Intro, page 68*

SPEAKING

Grammar: Subject and object pronouns
(10 minutes)

1. Read the information about subject and object pronouns. Provide and elicit additional examples: *I do judo every day. I like it. My teacher is very interesting. I like her. My friends are a lot of fun. I go places with them on the weekends.*
2. Check comprehension of the information by asking questions: *What is the object pronoun for we? For she? For you?*

Skill Note

Point out that the object pronoun for *you* and *it* is the same as the subject pronoun. Provide more practice with the object pronouns. Call on a student and say a sentence with a noun as object, e.g., *I play soccer on Tuesdays.* Have the student replace the noun with a pronoun: *I play it on Tuesdays.* Continue until students have practiced all forms.

▶ *Listening and Speaking Intro, page 69*

A (10 minutes)

1. Direct students to complete the activity individually.
2. Have students compare their answers in pairs.
3. Go over the answers with the class.

> **Activity A Answers, p. 69**
> **1.** He
> **2.** them
> **3.** We
> **4.** her
> **5.** It
> **6.** I
> **7.** me
> **8.** us

B (10 minutes)

1. Read the first item. Elicit the completion (*it*).
2. Direct students to complete the activity individually.
3. Have students compare their answers in pairs.
4. Go over the answers with the class.

Activity B Answers, p. 69
1. it
2. She
3. them
4. her
5. they
6. they
7. us
8. You

C (5 minutes)

1. Read the first item in Activity A. Elicit the completion (*He*). Ask: *Is this a subject or object pronoun?* Have students write *S* above *He*.

2. Direct students to identify the subject pronouns and object pronouns individually.

3. Have students compare their answers in pairs.

4. Go over the answers with the class.

Activity C Answers, p. 69
Activity A sentences:
1. he - S
2. them - O
3. we - S
4. her - O
5. I - S; it - S
6. I - S
7. me - O
8. us - O
Activity B sentences:
1. I - S; it - O
2. she - S
3. I - S; them - O
4. I - S; I - S; her - O
5. they - S
6. they - S
7. we - S; us - O
8. I - S; you - O; you - S

▶ *Listening and Speaking Intro, page 70*

D (10 minutes)

1. Read the first item. Elicit the completion (*you*).

2. Direct students to complete the activity individually.

3. Have students compare their answers in pairs.

4. Go over the answers with the class. Have students practice the conversation in pairs.

Activity D Answers, p. 70
1. you
2. it
3. she
4. you
5. I
6. They
7. you
8. us

 For additional practice with subject and object pronouns, have students visit *Q Online Practice*.

Pronunciation: Reduced pronouns
(5 minutes)

 CD1, Track 40

1. Read the information about reduced pronouns.

2. Play the audio.

3. Check comprehension by asking questions: *Do we usually stress pronouns? What pronouns do we reduce?*

▶ *Listening and Speaking Intro, page 71*

A (10 minutes)
 CD1, Track 41

1. Direct students to complete the activity individually.

2. Play the audio so students can check their answers.

3. Go over the answers with the class.

4. Have students work in pairs to practice saying the conversations.

Activity A Answers, p. 71
1. him; he; him; him; He; he
2. her; her; them

B (10 minutes)

1. Direct students to complete the activity individually.

2. Call on students and elicit a few examples.

3. Have students share their sentences with a partner.

Activity B Answers, p. 71

Activity B Answers, p. 71
Answers will vary. Possible answers:
1. He is a student.
2. I like him.
3. I work with her.
4. I play soccer with them.

 For additional practice with reduced pronouns, have students visit *Q Online Practice*.

▶ *Listening and Speaking Intro, page 72*

Speaking Skill: Agreeing and disagreeing
(5 minutes)

◎ CD1, Track 42

1. Read the information about agreeing and disagreeing.

2. Play the audio.

3. Check comprehension: *What expression is used to agree with a positive opinion? What can you say to agree with a negative opinion? How can you disagree politely?*

A (10 minutes)

◎ CD1, Track 43

1. Play the audio and have students check *agree* or *disagree*.

2. Play the audio again and have students write the expressions they hear.

3. Have students compare their answers with a partner.

4. Go over the answers with the class.

Activity A Answers, p. 72
1. Agree; Me too.
2. Disagree; I'm not sure.
3. Disagree; Oh, I don't know.
4. Agree; I don't either.
5. Agree; I do too.
6. Agree; Me neither.

▶ *Listening and Speaking Intro, page 73*

B (10 minutes)

1. Have students work individually to complete the sentences.

2. Go over the example conversation.

3. Have students take turns reading their sentences and agreeing or disagreeing.

4. Call on students to share their ideas with the class.

Activity B Answers, p. 73
Answers will vary. Possible answers:
1. I really like to see movies.
2. I don't like to play tennis.
3. I think skiing is fun.
4. I think television is boring.
5. I enjoy playing soccer.
6. I hate driving in traffic.

 For additional practice with agreeing and disagreeing, have students visit *Q Online Practice*.

Unit Assignment:
Participate in a group discussion about fun places in your area

Unit Question (5 minutes)

Refer students back to the ideas they discussed at the beginning of the unit about what makes something fun. Cue students if necessary by asking specific questions about the content of the unit: *What fun places are in a park? What do you like to do for fun? Who do you like to do fun things with?*

Learning Outcome

1. Tie the Unit Assignment to the unit Learning Outcome. Say: *The outcome for this unit is to participate in a group discussion about fun places in your area. This Unit Assignment is going to let you show your skill in discussing the top five fun places in your area, as well as agreeing or disagreeing with the members of your group.*

2. Explain that you are going to use a rubric similar to their Self-Assessment checklist on p. 74 to grade their Unit Assignment. You can also share a copy of the Unit Assignment Rubric (on p. 46 of this *Teacher's Handbook*) with the students.

Consider the Ideas (15 minutes)

◎ CD1, Track 44

A (10 minutes)

1. Have students read the list of places.

2. Play the audio and direct students to check the boxes.

3. Have students compare their answers with a partner.

4. Go over the answers with the class.

Activity A Answers, p. 73
Check 1, 3, 6, 7, 8, 9

B (5 minutes)

1. Have students discuss the questions with a partner.

2. Call on students to share their ideas with the class.

> **Activity B Answers, p. 73**
> Answers will vary.

21ˢᵀ CENTURY SKILLS

Being able to collaborate with other members of a group is an important skill in both academic and professional settings. In this Unit Assignment, students have to reach a consensus on the five best places. To reach a consensus as a group, members have to be able to express their opinions, agree and disagree politely, and sometimes put aside individual preferences in order to help the group. When students are gathering ideas in Activity A, suggest they rank their places. Which places are they willing to compromise on? This will help them do Prepare and Speak Activity C.

▶ *Listening and Speaking Intro, page 74*

Prepare and Speak

Gather Ideas

A (10 minutes)

1. Have students work individually to complete the chart.

2. Call on students to share their ideas with the class.

Organize Ideas

B (10 minutes)

1. Go over the directions and the examples.

2. Have students practice different ways to share their ideas with a partner.

3. Walk around the room and provide help as needed.

Tip for Success (1 minute)

1. Read the tip aloud.

2. Encourage students to give suggestions using *How about...?* and *What about...?* as they share their ideas.

Speak

C (15 minutes)

1. Go over the directions.

2. Have students review the Self-Assessment checklist on p. 74 to note what they should include in their presentation. Suggest they review the vocabulary on p. 62 and the information on subject and object pronouns on p. 68 if helpful.

3. Seat students in small groups to share their ideas.

4. Use the Unit Assignment Rubric on p. 46 of this *Teacher's Handbook* to score each student's discussion.

5. Alternatively, have listeners in each group complete the Unit Assignment Rubric for the other members.

Check and Reflect

Check

A (5 minutes)

1. Direct students to read and complete the Self-Assessment checklist.

2. Ask for a show of hands for how many students gave all or mostly *yes* answers.

3. Congratulate them on their success. Discuss the steps they can take if an item on the checklist was difficult for them. For example, they can review that section of the unit and plan to practice it over the next week.

▶ *Listening and Speaking Intro, page 75*

Reflect

B (5 minutes)

1. Direct students to discuss the questions with a partner.

2. Elicit ideas from the class.

3. Ask students if the unit prepared them to participate in a group discussion about the most fun places in their area.

Track Your Success

1. Have students circle the words they have learned in this unit. Suggest that students go back through the unit to review any words they have forgotten.

2. Have students check the skills they have mastered. If students need more practice to feel confident about their proficiency in a skill, point out the page numbers and encourage them to review.

3. Read the Learning Outcome aloud. Ask students if they feel that they have met the outcome.

Unit Assignment Rubric

Student name: _____

Date: _____

Unit Assignment: *Have a group discussion about fun places in your area.*

20 points = Discussion element was completely successful (at least 90% of the time).
15 points = Discussion element was mostly successful (at least 70% of the time).
10 points = Discussion element was partially successful (at least 50% of the time).
 0 points = Discussion element was not successful.

Have a group discussion about fun places in your area.	20 points	15 points	10 points	0 points
Student's information was clear.				
Student used vocabulary from the unit.				
Student used subject and object pronouns correctly.				
Student used expressions for agreeing and disagreeing.				
Student used reduced words correctly.				

Total points: _____

Comments:

6

Unit QUESTION
What makes a good home?

Home

LISTENING • listening for opinions
VOCABULARY • compound nouns
GRAMMAR • prepositions of location
PRONUNCIATION • stress in compound nouns
SPEAKING • agreeing and disagreeing

LEARNING OUTCOME

Design your perfect home and present your design to the class.

▶ *Listening and Speaking Intro, page 77*

Preview the Unit

Learning Outcome

1. Ask for a volunteer to read the unit skills and then the unit Learning Outcome.

2. Explain: *Your goal for the unit is to be able to design your perfect home and present your design to the class. I will use this Learning Outcome to grade your work at the end of the unit. Focus on learning these skills: Listening, Vocabulary, Grammar, Pronunciation, Speaking. They will help you reach your goal.*

A (10 minutes)

1. Say each word in the box and have students repeat.

2. Put students in pairs or small groups to complete the activity and discuss their answers.

3. Call on volunteers to share their ideas with the class. If anyone says that *hotel* should not be crossed out, explain that places to live are on a long-term basis.

4. Ask questions: *How many of you live in an apartment? Do you like it? Where do most people in the class live?*

Activity A Answers, p. 77
1. Crossed out: garage, hotel, office, park, restaurant
2. Answers will vary. Possible answer: I live in a small apartment. It's nice.

MULTILEVEL OPTION

Group lower-level students and allow them to use their dictionaries to look up the words in the box. Brainstorm a list of adjectives, or review some from Unit 3, to aid students with their descriptions. Have higher-level students write two additional sentences about where they live. Put students in pairs to share their sentences. Ask volunteers to write their sentences on the board.

B (5 minutes)

1. Focus students' attention on the photo. Have a volunteer describe the photo to the class.

2. Read the questions aloud. For the second question, *Which buildings look like good places to live in?*, suggest that students think about the features that they would like, such as a good view, a roof garden, a balcony, a yard, or a place to park a car, as well as features they would not like, such as buildings too close to one another, noise from people and traffic, etc.

3. Ask additional questions: *Where do you think this is? Why do you think so?*

Activity B Answers, p. 77
Answers will vary. Possible answers:
1. Houses, apartments buildings, modern buildings, historic buildings, office buildings.
2. The smaller buildings or houses are good places to live. I like living in historic houses, not apartment buildings.

C (15 minutes)

1. Introduce the Unit Question: "What makes a good home?" Ask related information questions or questions about personal experience: *How big is a good home? What rooms does it need? Does it need a yard?* Remind students to draw on their answers from Activities A and B.

2. Put students in small groups and give each group a piece of poster paper and a marker.

3. Read the Unit Question aloud. Give students a minute to silently consider their answers to the question. Tell students to pass the paper and the marker around the group. Direct each group member to write a different answer to the question. Encourage students to help one another.

4. Ask each group to choose a reporter to read the answers to the class. Point out similarities and differences among the answers. If answers from different groups are similar, make a group list that incorporates all of the answers. Post the list to refer to later in the unit.

> **Activity C Answers, p. 77**
> Answers will vary. Possible answers: Large. A good home is large. A good home has to be the right size for the people in it.

The Q Classroom

 CD2, Track 2

1. Play *The Q Classroom*. Use the example from the audio to help students continue the conversation. Ask: *What did the students say? Which one wants a large home?*

2. Ask additional questions: *Do you live alone or with people? If you live with people, who are they? Do you like a quiet home or a noisy home? Is location a good reason to choose a home?*

▶ *Listening and Speaking Intro, page 78*

LISTENING

LISTENING 1: How Do You Like Your Home?

VOCABULARY (10 minutes)

1. Model the activity. Read the first sentence. Elicit which answer is correct (*b*).

2. Direct students to read the sentences individually and circle *a* or *b*.

3. Have students compare their answers with a partner.

4. Go over the answers with the class.

Tip for Success (1 minute)

1. Read the tip aloud.

2. Elicit ideas for places students think of as "home."

> **MULTILEVEL OPTION**
>
> Group lower-level students and assist them with the task. Allow them to look the bold words up in their dictionaries. Have higher-level students complete the activity individually and then compare their answers with a partner. Tell the pairs to write an additional sample sentence for each expression. Have volunteers write one of their sentences on the board. Correct the sentences with the whole class, focusing on the use of the expression rather than on other grammatical issues.

> **Vocabulary Answers, p. 78**
> **1.** b   **2.** a
> **3.** b   **4.** a
> **5.** b   **6.** a
> **7.** a   **8.** b

For additional practice with the vocabulary, have students visit *Q Online Practice*.

PREVIEW LISTENING 1 (5 minutes)

1. Go over the directions and examples. Direct students to complete the activity individually.

2. Have students compare their answers with a partner.

3. Tell students they should review their answers after listening.

> **Preview Listening 1 Answers, p. 79**
> Answers will vary. Possible answers:
> Good: It's close to school. The rent is cheap.
> Bad: It's far from my family. My neighbors are unfriendly.

Listening 1 Background Note

At some colleges and universities, it is possible to get a private room, but it usually costs extra. Dorm rooms usually fit from one to four people. Some dorms are suite style, which means there is a common living area, shared bathroom, and sometimes a kitchen.

Comprehension Check

 CD2, Track 3

A (10 minutes)

1. Direct students' attention to the pictures. Ask: *What places do you see?*

2. Play the audio and have students complete the activity individually.

3. Have students compare their answers with a partner.

4. Go over the answers with the class.

> **Activity A Answers, p. 79**
> **1.** John, Dislikes
> **2.** Mary, Likes
> **3.** Carlos, Likes

B (15 minutes)

1. Go over the directions and statements in the box.

2. Direct students to write the good points and the bad points in the correct part of the chart.

3. Have students compare their answers with a partner.

4. Play the audio from Activity A again and have students check the correct name.

5. Go over the answers with the class.

> **Activity B Answers, p. 80**
> Good points:
> **1.** I don't pay any rent: Carlos
> **2.** It's comfortable: Mary
> **3.** It's near school and classes: John, Mary
> **4.** It's near public transportation: Carlos
> **5.** I like the people I live with: John, Carlos
> **6.** It's very private: Mary
> Bad points:
> **7.** The rent is expensive: Mary
> **8.** It's noisy: John, Carlos
> **9.** It's far from school: Carlos
> **10.** It's not private: John

C (5 minutes)

1. Have students discuss their answers with a partner.

2. Call on students to share their ideas with the class.

> **Activity C Answers, p. 80**
> Answers will vary. Possible answer: I like Mary's home because I like quiet, and I like to be alone.

Q WHAT DO YOU THINK?

Critical Thinking Tip (1 minute)

1. Read the tip aloud.

2. Point out that when we rank things, we use our knowledge and our opinions to make decisions.

A (5 minutes)

1. Direct students to first check the five sentences that are most important to them.

2. Students then rank the sentences from 1 to 5.

> **Activity A Answers, p. 81**
> Answers will vary.

B (5 minutes)

1. Have students compare their answers with a partner.

2. Call on each pair to share their answers with the class.

> **Activity B Answers, p. 81**
> Answers will vary.

Critical Q: Expansion Activity

Rank

1. Point out that sometimes we evaluate something on its own, and sometimes we evaluate it compared to other things. When we rank or prioritize something, we are evaluating things compared to other things.

2. Have students work in pairs to put the ideas in Activity A in order of importance, with 1 being the most important thing in a home.

3. Have each pair join another pair to compare their ideas.

4. Call on students to share their ideas with the class.

Learning Outcome

Use the Learning Outcome to frame the purpose and relevance of Listening 1. Say: *The Learning Outcome is to design your perfect home and present your design to the class. What did you learn from Listening 1? How will it help you present ideas about a home?*

(Students learned vocabulary for talking about features of homes, and they discussed what is important to them.)

Listening Skill: Listening for opinions (5 minutes)

🔊 CD2, Track 4

1. Have students read the information. Remind them that they already know from Unit 3 that *I think (that)* is for giving an opinion.

2. Play the audio.

3. Check comprehension by asking questions: *What is an opinion? What is one way to introduce an opinion? What are some verbs that show opinions? What are some adjectives that show opinions?*

▶ *Listening and Speaking Intro, page 82*

Activity (10 minutes)
🔊 CD2, Track 5

1. Have students read the sentences.

2. Play the audio and direct students to check the opinions they hear.

3. Have students compare their answers with a partner. Play the audio again if necessary.

4. Go over the answers with the class.

Listening Skill Answers, p. 82

1. Checked: Rob and Sam like the location. They think the rent is good.
2. Checked: Mary doesn't like taking the bus. Mary doesn't like her neighbors.
3. Checked: Matt likes James's new house. James thinks that there aren't a lot of bedrooms.
4. Checked: Kate doesn't like the living room in her new apartment. Mika thinks the apartment is in a good location.

▶ *Listening and Speaking Intro, page 83*

LISTENING 2: Housing Problems, Housing Solutions

VOCABULARY (10 minutes)

1. Direct students to read the definitions. Then read the first sentence and elicit the completion (*condition*).

2. Have students complete the activity individually.

3. Have students compare their answers with a partner.

4. Go over the answers with the class.

MULTILEVEL OPTION

Group lower-level students and assist them with the task. Provide example sentences to help them understand the words: *My rent is very **affordable**. It is a very small amount of money./The **condition** of the apartment was very good. It was clean and many things were new./There is a big **demand** for fresh vegetables in the city, but they are hard to find./This year is very dry. There is a water **shortage** now.*

Have higher-level students complete the activity individually and then compare answers with a partner. Tell the pairs to write an additional sample sentence for each expression. Have volunteers write one of their sentences on the board. Correct the sentences with the whole class, focusing on the words rather than on other grammatical aspects.

Vocabulary Answers, p. 83

1. condition	2. landlord
3. affordable	4. shortage
5. Housing	6. increase
7. demand	8. entertainment

 For additional practice with the vocabulary, have students visit *Q Online Practice*.

Listening and Speaking Intro, page 84

PREVIEW LISTENING 2 (5 minutes)

1. Direct students' attention to the picture. Ask: *Who do you see in the big picture? What is the man doing? Where is he?*

2. Go over the information about the listening. Have students check possible problems.

3. Tell students they should review their answers after listening.

> **Preview Listening 2 Answers, p. 84**
> Checked:
> There are not many dormitories.
> Many apartments aren't affordable for students.
> Some inexpensive housing is in bad condition.

Listening 2 Background Note

Colleges and universities handle the issue of student housing in different ways. Some universities have many dorms and require students to live on campus. Some have only a few dorms. They may guarantee on-campus housing only for the first year or two, and then students have to find their own.

Comprehension Check

 CD2, Track 6

A (10 minutes)

1. Play the audio and have students check the housing choices they hear.

2. Have students compare their answers with a partner.

3. Go over the answers with the class.

> **Activity A Answers, p. 84**
> a, b, e

Listening and Speaking Intro, page 85

B (10 minutes)

1. Have students read the statements.

2. Play the audio again and have students write *T* or *F*.

3. Have students compare their answers with a partner.

4. Go over the answers with the class.

5. For an added challenge, have students rewrite the false statements to make them true.

Activity B Answers, p. 85
1. F; The new campus is small.
2. T
3. T
4. T
5. T
6. F; Some students can live at home with families.
7. T
8. F; The city wants the university to grow.

EXPANSION ACTIVITY: Pros and Cons (10 minutes)

1. Put students in pairs or small groups to list the housing options available for students at their school or at a school in their area.

2. For each option, have students list three pros and three cons.

3. Call on students to share their ideas with the class or have each pair join another pair to compare their ideas.

WHAT DO YOU THINK?

A (5 minutes)

1. Direct students to complete the activity individually.

2. Have students discuss their ideas with a partner.

> **Activity A Answers, p. 85**
> Answers will vary. Possible answers:
> Best option: Some students share houses near campus with their friends.
> Reason 1: It's safe.
> Reason 2: It's close to school.
> Reason 3: It's fun.

B (minutes)

1. Seat students in pairs or small groups.

2. Tell students that they should think about both Listening 1 and Listening 2 as they discuss the questions in B.

3. Call on each pair to share their ideas with the class.

> **Activity B Answers**
> Answers will vary. Possible answers:
> 1. comfortable, affordable, safe
> 2. expensive, dangerous neighborhood, bad roommates

Learning Outcome

Use the Learning Outcome to frame the purpose and relevance of Listenings 1 and 2 and the Critical Q activity. Say: *The Learning Outcome is to design a perfect home and present your design to the class. What did you learn from Listening 2? How will it help you give a presentation about a home?*

(Students learned to talk about housing options.)

▶ *Listening and Speaking Intro, page 86*

Building Vocabulary: Compound nouns (5 minutes)

1. Have students read the information.

2. Check comprehension: *How many words make up a compound noun? What is an example of a one-word compound noun? What is an example of a two-word compound noun?*

Skill Note

If your students keep a vocabulary notebook, suggest they make three columns for compound nouns: one for one-word compounds, one for hyphenated compounds (e.g., mother-in-law), and one for two-word compounds. Whenever you come across a compound word in class, remind students to write it in their notebooks.

A (5 minutes)

1. Direct students to circle the compound nouns individually.

2. Have students compare their answers in pairs.

3. Go over the answers with the class.

> **Activity A Answers, p. 86**
> **1.** driveway
> **2.** bedrooms, bathrooms
> **3.** Swimming pool, backyard
> **4.** fireplace
> **5.** mailbox, post office
> **6.** smoke alarm, living room
> **7.** drugstore
> **8.** bookshelf, dining room

Tip for Success (1 minute)

1. Read the tip aloud. Remind students that noncount nouns are never plural.

2. Have students make each example word in the Building Vocabulary box plural.

3. Go over some plural compound nouns with the class: *shopping malls, police officers, living rooms.*

B (10 minutes)

1. Direct students to write the compound noun next to the definition.

2. Have students compare their answers with a partner.

3. Go over the answers with the class.

> **Activity B Answers, p. 86**
> **1.** post office
> **2.** bookshelf
> **3.** driveway
> **4.** fireplace
> **5.** backyard
> **6.** drugstore
> **7.** shopping mall
> **8.** streetcar

 For additional practice with compound nouns, have students visit *Q Online Practice.*

▶ *Listening and Speaking Intro, page 87*

Pronunciation: Stress in compound nouns (2 minutes)

CD2, Track 7

1. Have students read the information.

2. Play the audio.

3. Check comprehension by asking questions: *Which word do you usually stress in a compound noun, the first or the second?*

A (10 minutes)

CD2 Track 8

1. Play the audio and have students complete the activity individually.

2. Have students compare their answers with a partner.

3. Go over the answers with the class.

> **Activity A Answers, p. 87**
> **1.** a   **2.** a   **3.** a   **4.** b   **5.** b
> **6.** a   **7.** b   **8.** b   **9.** a   **10.** a

B (5 minutes)

1. Direct students to write their sentences individually.
2. Have students read their sentences to a partner.
3. Call on students to read their sentences to the class.

> **Activity B Answers, p. 87**
> Answers will vary. Possible answers:
> **1.** I want a house with a swimming pool.
> **2.** My apartment has two bedrooms.
> **3.** I park my car in the driveway.
> **4.** My apartment has a small living room.

 For additional practice with stress in compound nouns, have students visit *Q Online Practice*.

▶ *Listening and Speaking Intro, page 88*

SPEAKING

Grammar: Prepositions of location
Part 1 (5 minutes)

1. Have students read the information silently.
2. Check comprehension by asking questions: *What question do prepositions of location answer? When do we use* in? *When do we use* on? *When do we use* at?

Skill Note

We also use *in* with states or provinces. We also use *on* with the floors of a building. *At* is used with certain expressions: *at home, at school, at work.*

A (5 minutes)

1. Direct students to circle the correct preposition individually.
2. Have students compare their answers with a partner.
3. Go over the answers with the class.

> **Activity A Answers, p. 88**
> **1.** at
> **2.** in
> **3.** on
> **4.** at
> **5.** on
> **6.** in

B (10 minutes)

1. Model the activity. Read the first question and then answer it for yourself.
2. Direct students to answer the questions individually.
3. Have students practice asking and answering the question with a partner.
4. Call on students and ask a question.

> **Activity B Answers, p. 88**
> Answers will vary. Possible answers:
> **1.** I live in Mexico.
> **2.** I live in Puebla.
> **3.** I live on Marcos Street.
> **4.** I live at 142 Marcos Street.

▶ *Listening and Speaking Intro, page 89*

Grammar: Prepositions of location
Part 2 (5 minutes)

1. Have students read the information silently.
2. Check comprehension by asking questions: *Where is the bank? Is the gift shop across from the library? Where is the parking lot? What is between the bank and the gift shop?*

A (10 minutes)

1. Direct students to complete the sentences with the correct preposition individually.
2. Have students compare their answers with a partner.
3. Go over the answers with the class.

> **Activity A Answers, pp. 89–90**
> **1.** next to
> **2.** on the corner of
> **3.** behind
> **4.** between
> **5.** across from
> **6.** behind
> **7.** on the corner of
> **8.** next to
> **9.** across (the street) from
> **10.** on the corner of

▶ *Listening and Speaking Intro, page 90*

B (10 minutes)

1. Go over the example.
2. Direct students to find and correct the errors individually.
3. Have students compare their answers in pairs.
4. Go over the answers with the class.

2. The bookstore is <u>on</u> the corner of Central Avenue and Oak Street.
3. The library is <u>between</u> the bank and the gift shop.
4. The bank is across the street <u>from</u> Jackson Park.
5. The playground is <u>behind</u> Jackson Park.
6. The theater is next <u>to</u> the coffee shop.

C (10 minutes)

1. Model the activity. Tell the class about something in your city using *on the corner of*.
2. Direct students to write sentences individually.
3. Have students compare their ideas in pairs.
4. Elicit ideas from the class.

Activity B Answers, p. 90
Answers will vary. Possible answers:
1. The drugstore is on the corner of Market Street and 1st Street.
2. I live across the street from the market.
3. The park is behind the library.
4. The post office is between the library and the bank.
5. The hospital is next to the police station.

 For additional practice with prepositions of location, have students visit *Q Online Practice*.

▶ *Listening and Speaking Intro, page 91*

Q Unit Assignment: Design a home and give a presentation

Unit Question (5 minutes)

Refer students back to the ideas they discussed at the beginning of the unit about what makes a good home. Have students review the posters with their ideas on the wall. Cue students if necessary by asking specific questions about the content of the unit: *Where did the students in Listening 1 live? What did they like or dislike about their homes? What were some problems with housing for students in Jackson (Listening 2)? What are some adjectives that describe a good home? What are some places you want near your home?*

Learning Outcome

1. Tie the Unit Assignment to the unit Learning Outcome. Say: *The outcome for this unit is to design a perfect home and present your design to the class. This Unit Assignment is going to let you show your skill in giving a presentation and discussing the things you want in a perfect home.*

2. Explain that you are going to use a rubric similar to their Self-Assessment checklist on p. 92 to grade their Unit Assignment. You can also share a copy of the Unit Assignment Rubric (on p. 56 of this *Teacher's Handbook*) with the students.

Consider the Ideas (10 minutes)

🔊 CD 2, Track 9

1. Go over the ideas in the chart.
2. Play the audio and have students check the ideas they hear.
3. Go over the answers with the class.

Consider the Ideas Answers, p. 91
Checked: four bedrooms, three bathrooms, a big living room, a big window, a big backyard, a table with chairs, trees and flowers, a swimming pool, across the street from a park, good public transportation, near a supermarket, nice neighbors

Prepare and Speak

Gather Ideas

A (10-15 minutes)

1. Go over the directions.
2. Seat students in groups of three to complete their own charts.
3. Elicit ideas from the group.

21ST CENTURY SKILLS

Working creatively as a member of a team will help students in academic and professional settings. In some cases, the teams they will work on will already have defined roles. Defining roles can help any team work more smoothly. Suggest students designate roles for this group presentation. The group leader can make sure everyone expresses his or her ideas. The note-taker can write down all their ideas. The manager can make sure they get everything done on time.

Skill Review: Agreeing and disagreeing
(5 minutes)

1. Go over the information about agreeing and disagreeing.

2. Point out that students will be discussing their ideas as a group and that expressing their opinions politely will help them work together better.

3. Remind students to refer to p. 72 for more review.

▶ *Listening and Speaking Intro, page 92*

Organize Ideas

B (15 minutes)

1. Go over the directions and the steps.

2. Have the groups draw maps of their perfect homes, decide who will describe certain parts of the home, and practice the presentations.

3. Walk around the room and provide help as needed.

Speak

C (20 minutes)

1. Have students review the Self-Assessment checklist on p. 92 to note what they should include in their presentations.

2. Use the Unit Assignment Rubric on p. 56 of this *Teacher's Handbook* to score each student's part of the presentation.

3. Alternatively, have each group join another group and have students present to the other group. Have listeners complete the Unit Assignment Rubric.

Check and Reflect

Check

A (5 minutes)

1. Direct students to read and complete the Self-Assessment checklist.

2. Ask for a show of hands for how many students gave all or mostly *yes* answers.

3. Congratulate them on their success. Discuss the steps they can take if an item on the checklist was difficult for them.

▶ *Listening and Speaking Intro, page 93*

Reflect

B (5 minutes)

1. Direct students to discuss the questions with a partner.

2. Elicit ideas from the class.

3. Ask students if the unit prepared them to give a presentation on a home they would want to live in.

Track Your Success

1. Have students circle the words they have learned in this unit. Suggest that students go back through the unit to review any words they have forgotten.

2. Have students check the skills they have mastered. If students need more practice to feel confident about their proficiency in a skill, point out the page numbers and encourage them to review.

3. Read the Learning Outcome aloud. Ask students if they feel that they have met the outcome.

Unit Assignment Rubric

Student name: _____

Date: _____

Unit Assignment: *Design a home and give a presentation.*

20 points = Presentation element was completely successful (at least 90% of the time).
15 points = Presentation element was mostly successful (at least 70% of the time).
10 points = Presentation element was partially successful (at least 50% of the time).
 0 points = Presentation element was not successful.

Give a presentation	20 points	15 points	10 points	0 points
Student's information was clear.				
Student used vocabulary from the unit.				
Student used prepositions of location correctly.				
Student understood the opinions of group members.				
Student agreed and disagreed with opinions appropriately.				

Total points: _____

Comments:

Unit QUESTION
How does the weather affect you?

Weather

LISTENING • listening for opinions
VOCABULARY • nouns and adjectives for weather
GRAMMAR • adverbs of frequency
PRONUNCIATION • stressing important words
SPEAKING • asking for repetition

LEARNING OUTCOME

Participate in a group discussion about weather.

▶ *Listening and Speaking Intro, page 95*
Preview the Unit

Learning Outcome

1. Ask for a volunteer to read the unit skills and then the unit Learning Outcome.

2. Explain: *Your goal for the unit is to be able to participate in a group discussion about weather. I will use this Learning Outcome to grade your work at the end of the unit. Focus on learning these skills: Listening, Vocabulary, Grammar, Pronunciation, Speaking. They will help you reach your goal.*

A (5 minutes)

1. Say each word in the box and have students repeat.

2. Have students circle the words for weather and then discuss their answers with a partner.

3. Call on volunteers to share their ideas with the class. Ask questions: *Is the sun out today? Is there rain today? Do you like cold weather?*

> **Activity A Answers, p. 95**
> Circled: rain, lightning, warm, cold, hot, thunder, wind, sun, cloud, storm, snow

MULTILEVEL OPTION

Group lower-level students and go over the words in the box. Allow students to use their dictionaries if necessary. Have higher-level students work in pairs to identify which weather words are nouns and which are adjectives. Then have them write the adjective forms for the nouns. Ask volunteers to put the adjective forms on the board.

B (5 minutes)

1. Focus students' attention on the photo. Have a volunteer describe the photo to the class. Read the questions aloud.

2. Ask additional questions: *Do you like this kind of weather? How do the people feel? Why do you think so?*

> **Activity B Answers, p. 95**
> Answers will vary. Possible answers:
> Rain. It's raining. It's windy and rainy.
> Walking outside. The people are walking on the street. The people are walking on the street and their umbrellas are blowing in the wind.

C (15 minutes)

1. Introduce the Unit Question: "How does the weather affect you?" Ask related information questions or questions about personal experience: *What kind of weather do you like? Why? What kind of weather do we have at this time of year? Do you like it?* Remind students to draw on their answers from Activities A and B.

2. Put students in small groups and give each group a piece of poster paper and a marker.

3. Read the Unit Question aloud. Give students a minute to silently consider their answers to the question. Tell students to pass the paper and the marker around the group. Direct each group member to write a different answer to the question. Encourage students to help one another.

4. Ask each group to choose a reporter to read the answers to the class. Point out similarities and differences among the answers. If answers from different groups are similar, make a group list that incorporates all of the answers. Post the list to refer to later in the unit.

Activity C Answers, p. 95
Answers will vary. Possible answers:
I feel cold. It can make me cold. I wear warm clothes when the weather is cold.

The Q Classroom
 CD2, Track 10

1. Play *The Q Classroom*. Use the example from the audio to help students continue the conversation. Ask: *What did the students say? Do they all like the same kind of weather?*

2. Relate the conversation to personal experience. Ask: *Who has the same ideas as you?*

▶ *Listening and Speaking Intro, page 96*

LISTENING

LISTENING 1: The World of Weather

VOCABULARY (10 minutes)

1. Direct students to read the definitions and then complete the sentences individually.

2. Have students compare their answers with a partner.

3. Go over the answers with the class.

Tip for Success (1 minute)

1. Read the tip aloud.

2. Suggest students remember that *a* is for *action*, so *affect* is the verb.

MULTILEVEL OPTION

Group lower-level students and assist them with the task. Provide alternate example sentences to help them understand the words. *The amount of rain* **affects** *the plants./One* **effect** *of eating too much is weight gain./The mail isn't here yet. There's some kind of* **delay**.*/The consequences of cheating are* **severe**. *You will fail the class.*

Have higher-level students complete the activity individually and then compare their answers with a partner. Tell the pairs to write an additional sample sentence for each expression. Have volunteers write one of their sentences on the board. Correct the sentences with the whole class, focusing on the use of the word rather than on other grammatical issues.

Vocabulary Answers, p. 96
1. severe
2. power
3. flood
4. temperature
5. delay
6. effect
7. cause
8. affect

web For additional practice with the vocabulary, have students visit *Q Online Practice*.

▶ *Listening and Speaking Intro, page 97*

Tip for Success (1 minute)

1. Read the tip aloud.

2. Direct students to use *it's* in the Preview activity.

PREVIEW LISTENING 1 (10 minutes)

1. Direct students' attention to the weather map. Ask questions: *What is the weather like in China? In Japan? In the eastern United States?*

2. Have students talk about the weather today in pairs.

3. Tell students they should review their answers after listening.

Preview Listening 1 Answers, p. 97
Answers will vary. Possible answers:
It's cold. It's rainy and windy.

Skill Review: Listening for opinions
(5 minutes)

1. Have students read the skill review about listening for opinions.

2. Suggest students take notes on the adjectives they hear that give opinions.

Listening 1 Background Note

Temperatures can be in either Celsius or Fahrenheit. Most people around the world, and scientists everywhere, use the Celsius scale. The United States and Belize are two countries that prefer Fahrenheit. Some countries such as Canada use both scales. The Celsius scale also used to be called Centigrade.

Tip for Success (1 minute)

1. Read the tip aloud.

2. Elicit ideas from the class as to what they think the temperature might be in different cities.

Comprehension Check

A (10 minutes)
🔊 CD2, Track 11

1. Direct students' attention to the chart and have them read the names of the places.

2. Play the audio and have students complete the activity individually.

3. Have students compare their answers with a partner.

4. Go over the answers with the class.

> **Activity A Answers, p. 97**
> **2.** Bad weather
> **3.** Bad weather
> **4.** Bad weather
> **5.** Good weather
> **6.** Good weather
> **7.** Good weather
> **8.** Good weather
> **9.** Bad weather
> **10.** Good weather

▶ *Listening and Speaking Intro, page 98*

Tip for Success (1 minute)

1. Read the tip aloud.

2. Have students read the sentences and answers in Activity B before they listen.

B (10 minutes)
🔊 CD2, Track 11

1. Play the audio and have students complete the activity individually.

2. Have students compare their answers with a partner.

3. Go over the answers with the class.

> **Activity B Answers, p. 98**
> **1.** b
> **2.** d
> **3.** b
> **4.** a
> **5.** b
> **6.** a

Q WHAT DO YOU THINK?

1. Go over the questions.

2. Put students in pairs to discuss their answers.

3. Call on each pair or group to share their answers with the class.

> **What Do You Think? Answers, p. 98**
> Answers will vary. Possible answers:
> **1.** I like warm, sunny weather. I like to be outdoors.
> **2.** I don't like rainy weather. I can't ride my bike in the rain.
> **3.** Snow causes problems for me. I don't like to drive in the snow.

Learning Outcome

Use the Learning Outcome to frame the purpose and relevance of Listening 1. Say: *The Learning Outcome is to participate in a group discussion about the weather. What did you learn from Listening 1? How will it help you talk about how the weather affects you?*

(Students learned vocabulary for weather situations and problems.)

▶ *Listening and Speaking Intro, page 99*

LISTENING 2: Weather and Our Moods

VOCABULARY (10 minutes)

1. Direct students to read the sentences and circle *a* or *b*.

2. Have students compare their answers with a partner.

3. Go over the answers with the class.

> **MULTILEVEL OPTION**
>
> Group lower-level students and assist them with the task. Direct them to identify the clues in the sentences that help them with the meaning. For example, in the first sentence, the clues are: *Don't talk to John* and *failed his exam.* Ask: *Is he a bad student? Does he feel bad?* Allow students to use a dictionary if necessary.
>
> Have higher-level students complete the activity individually and then compare their answers with a partner. Tell the pairs to write an additional sample sentence for each expression. Have volunteers write one of their sentences on the board. Correct the sentences with the whole class, focusing on the use of the words rather than on other grammatical issues.

Vocabulary Answers, p. 99
1. a
2. a
3. a
4. b
5. a
6. b
7. a
8. a

 For additional practice with the vocabulary, have students visit *Q Online Practice*.

▶ *Listening and Speaking Intro, page 100*

PREVIEW LISTENING 2 (5 minutes)

1. Go over the questions.
2. Put students in pairs or small groups to answer the questions.
3. Call on students to share their ideas with the class.
4. Tell students they should review their answers after listening.

Preview Listening 2 Answers, p. 100
Answers will vary. Possible answers:
1. It decreases.
2. I feel happy.
3. I feel sad.
4. I feel irritable when it's extremely hot or cold.

Listening 2 Background Note

Seasonal Affective Disorder (SAD) was first identified in the early 1980s by Dr. Norman Rosenthal at the National Institute of Mental Health in the United States. It affects more women than men and first appears in adolescence or adulthood. It can affect up to 10% of the population in places that have long, dark winters.

Comprehension Check

A (10 minutes)
 CD2, Track 12

1. Play the audio and have students check the weather choices they hear.
2. Have students compare their answers with a partner.
3. Go over the answers with the class.

Activity A Answers, p. 100
Checked: cold, dark winters; extremely hot summers; beautiful weather

B (10 minutes)
 CD2, Track 12

1. Direct students to read the statements.
2. Play the audio and have students write *T* or *F*.
3. Have students compare their answers with a partner.
4. Go over the answers with the class.
5. Read the third statement. Elicit ways to make the sentence true (for example, *Little sunlight causes SAD* or *Bright sunlight can help SAD*). Have students rewrite 3, 4, and 8 to make them true.

Activity B Answers, p. 100
1. T
2. T
3. F; People develop SAD during cold, dark winters.
4. F; There are six symptoms of SAD.
5. T
6. T
7. T
8. F; Extremely hot weather sometimes makes people irritable and angry.

▶ *Listening and Speaking Intro, page 101*

WHAT DO YOU THINK?

A (10 minutes)

1. Seat students in pairs.
2. Elicit the names of the seasons: *spring, summer, winter, fall/autumn.*
3. Call on each pair to share their ideas with the class.

> **MULTILEVEL OPTION**
>
> Group lower-level students. Provide or elicit a word bank (*spring, summer, fall, winter, skiing, swimming, running, soccer, rain, sun, wind, clouds, snow*). Have higher-level students answer an additional question: *What do you like to do in each season?*

Activity A Answers, p. 101
Answers will vary. Sample answers:
1. I like winter. I like to go skiing.
2. I don't like fall. It rains a lot in the fall.

B (5 minutes)

1. Tell students that they should think about both Listening 1 and Listening 2 as they discuss the questions in B.

2. Go over the example.

3. Direct students to complete the survey individually.

4. Have students compare their answers with a partner.

5. Call on students to share their ideas with the class.

> **Activity B Answers, p. 101**
> Answers will vary.

Learning Outcome

Use the Learning Outcome to frame the purpose and relevance of Listenings 1 and 2. Say: *The Learning Outcome is to participate in a group discussion about weather. What did you learn from Listening 2? How will it help you to talk with a group about how weather affects you?*

(Students learned specific ways weather can affect a person's mood.)

Building Vocabulary: Nouns and adjectives for weather (5 minutes)

1. Have students read the information about nouns and adjectives for weather.

2. Check comprehension: *What suffix or ending can you add to a weather noun to make it an adjective? If the noun is* sun, *what is the adjective?*

Skill Note

Point out that when the noun follows the pattern consonant-vowel-consonant (e.g., *sun*), students need to double the final consonant before adding *-y* (e.g., *sunny*).

▶ *Listening and Speaking Intro, page 102*

A (10 minutes)

1. Direct students to circle the correct form of the word.

2. Have students compare their answers with a partner.

3. Go over the answers with the class.

> **Activity A Answers, p. 102**
> **1.** cloud
> **2.** stormy
> **3.** sunny
> **4.** snow
> **5.** wind
> **6.** rainy
> **7.** foggy
> **8.** chill

B (10 minutes)

1. Direct students' attention to the photos and ask: *What do you see? What is the weather like?*

2. Have students complete the sentences individually.

3. Have students share their ideas with a group.

4. Call on students to share their ideas with the class.

> **Activity B Answers, p. 102**
> Answers will vary. Possible answers:
> **1.** snowy
> **2.** hot
> **3.** cool
> **4.** rainy

 For additional practice with nouns and adjectives for weather, have students visit *Q Online Practice*.

▶ *Listening and Speaking Intro, page 103*

SPEAKING

Grammar: Adverbs of frequency
(10 minutes)

1. Have students read the information about adverbs of frequency.

2. Elicit or provide additional example sentences: *It often rains in April. It never snows in August. We hardly ever swim on cold days.*

3. Check comprehension by asking questions: *Which adverb means 100 percent of the time? Which adverb means 0 percent of the time? Which adverb means maybe 40 percent of the time? Do adverbs come before the verb* be?

Skill Note

We usually use the simple present tense with adverbs of frequency to talk about situations in the general present.

EXPANSION ACTIVITY: Notice the Grammar
(10 minutes)

🔊 CD2, Track 12

1. Tell students to listen and write down all the adverbs of frequency they hear.

2. Play the audio for Listening 2.

3. Have students compare their answers with a partner. Play the audio again if necessary.

4. Elicit the answers from the class: *usually, often, usually, sometimes, sometimes, often, sometimes.*

A (5–10 minutes)

1. Go over the directions and the example.

2. Write another sentence on the board: *Never the winter is warm.* Elicit which word is the adverb (*never*). Ask students where it should go. (*The winter is never warm.*)

3. Have students correct the errors individually.

4. Have students compare their answers with a partner.

5. Go over the answers with the class.

> **Activity A Answers, p. 103**
> **2.** no error
> **3.** I often hear thunder in July.
> **4.** The winter is never warm.
> **5.** Brazil is never cold.
> **6.** We hardly ever have big storms.
> **7.** It is often very cold in Norway.
> **8.** no error

▶ *Listening and Speaking Intro, page 104*

B (10 minutes)

1. Direct students to write sentences individually.

2. Have students compare their answers with a partner.

3. Go over the answers with the class.

> **Activity B Answers, p. 104**
> **1.** It's usually very hot in August./Usually, it's very hot in August.
> **2.** I always feel tired in the winter.
> **3.** It hardly ever snows in November.
> **4.** There are never severe thunderstorms in June.
> **5.** It sometimes snows in the mountains in September./Sometimes, it snows in the mountains in September.

Tip for Success (1 minute)

1. Read the tip aloud.

2. Ask students to underline *ever* in the questions in Activity C.

C (15 minutes)

1. Direct students to answer the questions individually in complete sentences.

2. Have students compare their answers with a partner.

3. Elicit answers from the class.

4. Have students practice asking and answering the questions in pairs.

> **Activity C Answers, pp. 104–105**
> Answers will vary. Possible answers:
> **1.** No, I never stay home in very hot weather.
> **2.** Yes, I usually feel sad when it's cold and cloudy.
> **3.** Yes, I often feel tired when it's extremely hot.
> **4.** My city is hardly ever extremely hot in the summer.
> **5.** No, I never play sports in the winter.
> **6.** Yes, my city sometimes has floods.
> **7.** Yes, my city often loses power during storms.

 For additional practice with adverbs of frequency, have students visit *Q Online Practice.*

▶ *Listening and Speaking Intro, page 105*

Speaking Skill: Asking for repetition
(10 minutes)

🔊 CD2, Track 13

1. Have students read the information and example conversations.

2. Play the audio.

3. Check comprehension by asking: *What expressions can you use to ask for repetition? What do we ask people to repeat? What do we say if we don't understand the answer?*

▶ *Listening and Speaking Intro, page 106*

A (10 minutes)

🔊 CD2, Track 14

1. Direct students to listen and choose the best answer.

2. Play the audio.

3. Have students compare their answers with a partner.

4. Go over the answers with the class.

> **Activity A Answers, p. 106**
> **1.** b **2.** a **3.** d **4.** a

B (10–15 minutes)

1. Go over the example and the questions.
2. Put students in pairs and have them choose a city.
3. Have students take turns asking and answering questions about the city they chose. Remind them to ask for repetition.

Activity B Answers, p. 106
Answers will vary. Possible answers:
City: Tokyo, Japan
1. It's hot and dry in the summer.
2. It's cold and rainy in the winter.
3. It's about 26 degrees Celcius in the summer.
4. It's about 5 degrees Celcius in the winter.
5. My favorite season is spring. It is comfortable.

Critical Thinking Tip (1 minute)

1. Read the tip aloud.
2. Suggest students choose one thing they learn in each class and apply it during the week. For example, they could decide to practice certain vocabulary words, write a paragraph using a grammar point, or talk with someone about the unit ideas in English.

Critical Q: Expansion Activity

Apply

1. Point out that the questions in Activity B ask students to choose a city and then apply vocabulary and ideas they have about weather to answer the questions.
2. To help students think quickly, have students stand.
3. Ask a series of questions about weather and have students move around the room, repeating the question and going to stand with students who have the same answer.
What season is your favorite? Why? What weather do you like best? When do you like to go on vacation? What is your favorite outdoor activity? How do you feel in cold weather?
Remind students to ask for repetition if they don't understand their classmates' answers.
4. When students are standing in groups, call on someone in each group to share their ideas.

21ST CENTURY SKILLS

The ability to ask for repetition is a vital skill in the classroom and in future professional settings. Whether it is because a speaker is conveying ideas in another language or is providing information about an unfamiliar topic, students will sometimes need to ask a speaker to repeat himself/herself. Students are often hesitant to ask for repetition because they don't want to appear unqualified or ignorant. To help students become more comfortable with this skill, encourage them to practice with you. Occasionally read material aloud in English from other sources or talk about topics they haven't studied in class. Elicit appropriate requests for repetition.

 For additional practice with asking for repetition, have students visit *Q Online Practice*.

▶ *Listening and Speaking Intro, page 107*

Pronunciation: Stressing important words (5 minutes)

🔊 CD2, Track 15

1. Have students read the information and example conversations.
2. Play the audio.
3. Check comprehension by asking questions: *What are examples of important words? What are examples of words we usually stress?*

A (10 minutes)

🔊 CD2, Track 16

1. Direct students to underline the stressed words.
2. Play the audio and have students check their answers.
3. Go over the answers with the class.
4. Have students practice the conversation in pairs.

Activity A Answers, pp. 107–108
2. cold
3. hot, sunny
4. shopping, swimming
5. 40

B (5–10 minutes)

1. Direct students to answer the questions with complete sentences.

2. Have students circle the stressed words.

3. Call on students to share their answers with the class.

> **Activity B Answers, p. 108**
> Answers will vary. Possible answers:
> **1.** I like (warm) weather.
> **2.** I don't like (rainy) weather.
> **3.** (June) is my favorite month of the year.
> **4.** It's (warm) and (sunny) today.
> **5.** I want to go (swimming) and play (tennis).

C (5–10 minutes)

1. Put students in pairs to take turns asking and answering the questions in B.

2. Walk around the room to monitor the activity and give help as needed.

 For additional practice with stressing important words, have students visit *Q Online Practice*.

Unit Assignment: Participate in a group discussion about weather

Unit Question (5 minutes)

Refer students back to the ideas they discussed at the beginning of the unit about weather. Have students review the posters with their ideas on the wall. Cue students if necessary by asking specific questions about the content of the unit: *What are some problems weather causes? What vocabulary words do you know for weather, both nouns and adjectives? How does weather affect people?*

Learning Outcome

1. Tie the Unit Assignment to the unit Learning Outcome. Say: *The outcome for this unit is to participate in a group discussion about weather. This Unit Assignment is going to let you show your skill in talking about weather and how it affects you.*

2. Explain that you are going to use a rubric similar to their Self-Assessment checklist on p. 110 to grade their Unit Assignment. You can also share a copy of the Unit Assignment Rubric (on p. 66 of this *Teacher's Handbook*) with the students.

▶ *Listening and Speaking Intro, page 109*
Consider the Ideas (10 minutes)

CD2, Track 17

1. Direct students to read the sentences.

2. Play the audio and have students check the sentences they hear.

3. Have students compare their answers with a partner.

4. Go over the answers with the class.

> **Consider the Ideas Answers, p. 109**
> Checked: 2, 3, 5, 7, 8

Prepare and Speak

Gather Ideas

A (5–10 minutes)

1. Direct students' attention to the pictures. Ask: *What do you see?*

2. Have students complete the chart with their ideas.

3. Elicit ideas from the class.

▶ *Listening and Speaking Intro, page 110*
Organize Ideas

B (5–10 minutes)

1. Direct students to write sentences about five ideas from Activity A.

2. Have students share their ideas with a partner.

Speak

C (10 minutes)

1. Go over the directions and the steps.

2. Remind students to review the Self-Assessment checklist on p. 110. Refer students to pp. 96 and 99 to review vocabulary and to p. 103 for adverbs of frequency.

3. Put students into small groups to share their ideas about how weather affects them.

4. Call on students to share their ideas with the class.

5. Use the Unit Assignment Rubric on p. 66 of this *Teacher's Handbook* to score each student's participation.

6. Alternatively, have listeners in each group complete the Unit Assignment Rubric.

Check and Reflect

A (5 minutes)

1. Direct students to read and complete the Self-Assessment checklist.

2. Ask for a show of hands for how many students gave all or mostly *yes* answers.

3. Congratulate them on their success. Discuss the steps they can take if an item on the checklist was difficult for them. For example, they can review that section of the unit and plan to practice it over the next week.

Reflect

B (5 minutes)

1. Direct students to discuss the questions with a partner.

2. Elicit ideas from the class.

3. Ask students if the unit prepared them to participate in a group discussion about how the weather affects them.

Track Your Success

1. Have students circle the words they have learned in this unit. Suggest that students go back through the unit to review any words they have forgotten.

2. Have students check the skills they have mastered. If students need more practice to feel confident about their proficiency in a skill, point out the page numbers and encourage them to review.

3. Read the Learning Outcome aloud. Ask students if they feel that they have met the outcome.

Unit Assignment Rubric

Student name: _____

Date: _____

Unit Assignment: *Participate in a group discussion about weather.*

20 points = Discussion element was completely successful (at least 90% of the time).
15 points = Discussion element was mostly successful (at least 70% of the time).
10 points = Discussion element was partially successful (at least 50% of the time).
 0 points = Discussion element was not successful.

Participated in a group discussion about weather.	20 points	15 points	10 points	0 points
Student used vocabulary from this unit.				
Student used adverbs of frequency correctly.				
Student asked for repetition when necessary in the group discussion.				
Student showed comprehension of other people's opinions.				
Student used word stress correctly for important information.				

Total points: _____

Comments:

Unit QUESTION

What do you do to stay healthy?

Health

LISTENING • listening for frequency
VOCABULARY • adjectives ending in *-ed*
GRAMMAR • modals *can* and *should*
PRONUNCIATION • *can, can't, should,* and *shouldn't*
SPEAKING • asking for repetition

LEARNING OUTCOME

Create, conduct, and discuss a
health survey.

▶ *Listening and Speaking Intro, page 113*

Preview the Unit

Learning Outcome

1. Ask for a volunteer to read the unit skills and then the unit Learning Outcome.

2. Explain: *Your goal for the unit is to be able to create, conduct, and discuss a health survey. I will use this Learning Outcome to grade your work at the end of the unit. Focus on learning these skills: Listening, Vocabulary, Grammar, Pronunciation, Speaking. They will help you reach your goal.*

A (10 minutes)

1. Put students in pairs or small groups to complete the activity and discuss their answers.

2. Call on volunteers to share their ideas with the class. Ask questions: *Why is exercise healthy? Why is it not a good idea to watch a lot of television? How many of you worry a lot? What does worrying do to your health? Why is sugar unhealthy?*

Activity A Answers, p. 113
Answers will vary.

MULTILEVEL OPTION

Pair a higher-level student with a lower-level student to help with the vocabulary and to discuss their ideas.

B (5 minutes)

1. Focus students' attention on the photo. Have a volunteer describe the photo to the class. Read the questions aloud.

2. Ask additional questions: *Do you ride a bicycle to school? Is this a healthy activity? Why or why not?*

Activity B Answers, p. 113
Answers will vary. Possible answers: He is in a garage. He is going to ride a bike. He is going to work because he is wearing a suit. Riding a bike is good exercise and saves energy.

C (15 minutes)

1. Introduce the Unit Question: "What do you do to stay healthy?" Ask related information questions or questions about personal experience. Ask: *Do you care about what you eat? What activities are healthy? What activities are unhealthy? How often do you go to the doctor?* Remind students to draw on their answers from Activities A and B.

2. Put students in small groups and give each group a piece of poster paper and a marker.

3. Read the Unit Question aloud. Give students a minute to silently consider their answers to the question. Tell students to pass the paper and the marker around the group. Direct each group member to write a different answer to the question. Encourage students to help one another.

4. Ask each group to choose a reporter to read the answers to the class. Point out similarities and differences among the answers. If answers from different groups are similar, make a group list that incorporates all of the answers. Post the list to refer to later in the unit.

Activity C Answers, p. 113

Answers will vary. Possible answers:
Exercise. Exercise and eat healthy food. I exercise, eat healthy food, and drink a lot of water.

The Q Classroom

CD2, Track 18

1. Play *The Q Classroom*. Use the example from the audio to help students continue the conversation. Ask: *What did the students say? Who do you think has the healthiest habits? Who is the most like you?*

2. To help students relate this to their own experience, ask: *Do you exercise a lot? Do you get enough sleep? Is it bad to worry?*

► *Listening and Speaking Intro, page 114*

LISTENING

LISTENING 1: Health Watch

VOCABULARY (10 minutes)

1. Direct students to read the definitions and then complete the sentences individually.

2. Have students compare their answers with a partner.

3. Go over the answers with the class.

> **MULTILEVEL OPTION**
>
> Group lower-level students and assist them with the task. Provide alternate example sentences to help them understand the words. *I don't eat meat. I have a vegetarian **diet.**/ I have a lot of **energy**. I'm always ready to do something./ I **manage** my time very well. I make a schedule and get everything done. /Maria wants to **reduce** the amount of sugar she eats./Are you feeling **run-down**? You look very tired.*
>
> Have higher-level students complete the activity individually and then compare their answers with a partner. Tell the pairs to write an additional sample sentence for each expression. Have volunteers write one of their sentences on the board. Correct the sentences with the whole class, focusing on the use of the words rather than on other grammatical issues.

Vocabulary Answers, p. 114

1. lonely
2. reduce
3. stress
4. energy
5. diet
6. stressful
7. manage
8. run-down

 For additional practice with the vocabulary, have students visit *Q Online Practice*.

► *Listening and Speaking Intro, page 115*

PREVIEW LISTENING 1 (5 minutes)

1. Direct students' attention to the picture. Ask: *Who do you see? How does she feel? Does she have a problem?*

2. Go over the directions and have students check their answers and then compare their ideas with a partner.

3. Elicit additional ideas from the class.

4. Tell students they should review their answers after listening.

Preview Listening 1 Answers, p. 115

Checked: they have money problems; they work long hours; they want good grades; they are lonely

Listening 1 Background Note

Some popular ways to reduce stress, and therefore improve health, include yoga and meditation. Yoga dates back at least two thousand years and is believed to have begun in India. Yoga involves physical poses, stretching, and breathing. Meditation often involves deep breathing and visualization. Recent medical research suggests that meditation may not only reduce the effects of stress, but may help specific health problems such as high blood pressure, arthritis, and even infertility.

Comprehension Check

🔊 CD2, Track 19

A (10 minutes)

1. Direct students to read the list of topics.
2. Play the audio and have students complete the activity individually.
3. Have students compare their answers with a partner.
4. Go over the answers with the class.

> **Activity A Answers, p. 115**
> Circled: work, children, money, grades, sickness, exercise, food, friends

▶ *Listening and Speaking Intro, page 116*

Tip for Success (1 minute)

1. Read the tip aloud.
2. Have students find and circle the noun form in the chart.

B (10 minutes)

1. Direct students to read the sentences in the chart.
2. Play the audio and have students check the correct column individually.
3. Have students compare their answers with a partner. Play the audio again if necessary.
4. Go over the answers with the class.

> **Activity B Answers, p. 116**
> **1.** Symptoms of stress
> **2.** Ways to reduce stress
> **3.** Causes of stress
> **4.** Ways to reduce stress
> **5.** Causes of stress
> **6.** Symptoms of stress
> **7.** Causes of stress
> **8.** Ways to reduce stress
> **9.** Symptoms of stress
> **10.** Causes of stress

WHAT DO YOU THINK? (5–10 minutes)

1. Direct students to read the ideas in the chart. Go over the example conversation.
2. Have students add one idea to the chart and then check their answers.
3. Have students discuss their answers with a partner.

4. Call on each pair or group to share their answers with the class.

> **What Do You Think? Answers, p. 116**
> Answers will vary. Possible answers: I don't feel any stress with my friends. We do fun things together. I feel a lot of stress with my family. My parents want me to get good grades.

Learning Outcome

Use the Learning Outcome to frame the purpose and relevance of Listening 1. Say: *The Learning Outcome is to create, conduct, and discuss a health survey. What did you learn from Listening 1? How will it help you create questions for the survey?*

(Students learned about things that cause stress, the symptoms of stress, and ways to reduce stress.)

▶ *Listening and Speaking Intro, page 117*

Listening Skill: Listening for frequency
(5 minutes)

🔊 CD2, Track 20

1. Have students read the information in the box.
2. Play the audio and have students follow along.
3. Check comprehension by asking questions: *What does* frequency *mean? What are some adverbs of frequency? What are some expressions with* every*? What are some other expressions?*

A (10 minutes)
🔊 CD2, Track 21

1. Direct students' attention to the picture. Ask: *Who do you see? Which person do you think is healthier? Why?*
2. Play the audio and have students circle the expressions they hear.
3. Have students compare their answers with a partner.
4. Go over the answers with the class.

> **Activity A Answers, p. 117**
> **1.** always
> **2.** every day
> **3.** never
> **4.** six days a week
> **5.** sometimes, three times a week
> **6.** usually, twice a week
> **7.** usually, always
> **8.** three times a week

B (10 minutes)

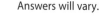 CD2, Track 22

1. Direct students to read the questions.

2. Play the audio and have students circle the answers individually.

3. Have students compare their answers with a partner.

4. Go over the answers with the class.

> **Activity B Answers, p. 118**
> **1.** c
> **2.** c
> **3.** b
> **4.** a
> **5.** b

C (10 minutes)

1. Direct students to read the questions.

2. Have students work in pairs to take turns asking and answering the questions.

3. Call on students to tell the class about one of their partner's answers.

> **Activity C Answers, p. 118**
> Answers will vary.

 For additional practice with listening for frequency, have students visit *Q Online Practice*.

◀ *Listening and Speaking Intro, page 119*

LISTENING 2: How Often Do You Work Out?

VOCABULARY (10 minutes)

1. Direct students to read the first sentence. Elicit the correct answer (*a*).

2. Have students read the sentences and circle the correct answers individually.

3. Have students compare their answers with a partner.

4. Go over the answers with the class.

MULTILEVEL OPTION

Group lower-level students and allow them to use their dictionaries. Have higher-level students work in pairs to write conversations in which they use at least four of the new expressions. Ask volunteers to perform their conversations for the class.

> **Vocabulary Answers, p. 119**
> **1.** a
> **2.** b
> **3.** b
> **4.** a
> **5.** b
> **6.** a
> **7.** a
> **8.** a

 For additional practice with the vocabulary, have students visit *Q Online Practice*.

◀ *Listening and Speaking Intro, page 120*

PREVIEW LISTENING 2 (10 minutes)

1. Direct students' attention to the chart. Ask: *What is one example of what people with good health habits do? What is the example for people with bad health habits?*

2. Have students complete the chart individually.

3. Have students compare their ideas with a partner.

4. Tell students they should review their answers after listening.

> **Preview Listening 2 Answers, p. 120**
> Answers will vary. Possible answers:
> People with good health habits....
> watch what they eat, exercise, sleep eight hours a night, don't work a lot
> People with bad health habits....
> eat junk food, work a lot, don't exercise, don't sleep enough

Critical Thinking Tip (1 minute)

1. Read the tip aloud.

2. Point out that sometimes the word *compare* means to look for things that are similar, and the word *contrast* means to look for things that are different. However, often the word *compare* means to look for both similarities and differences.

Critical Q: Expansion Activity

Compare

1. Point out that comparing two or more things can help us understand each thing more deeply.

2. To help students look more closely at one aspect of health, ask them to choose one of the following: two diets (for example, meat vs. vegetarian, or American vs. Chinese), two types of exercise (for example, swimming vs. soccer, or weight-training vs. running), or two types of schedules (day vs. night).

3. Have students work with a partner to complete a chart comparing the two things they chose.

4. Have each pair join another pair to share their ideas.

5. Call on students to share their ideas with the class.

Listening 2 Background Note

Recent research on sleep suggests that most people will be healthier if they sleep seven to eight hours a night. People who sleep much longer have a shorter life expectancy, and people who sleep much less experience more stress. The most common times to have a car accident because of falling asleep at the wheel are at 6:00 in the morning and 4:00 in the afternoon. Many people in the Mediterranean region sleep five or six hours at night and two hours in the afternoon.

Comprehension Check

 CD2, Track 23

A (10 minutes)

1. Play the audio. Ask students to read and complete the activity individually.

2. Have students compare their answers with a partner.

3. Go over the answers with the class.

> **Activity A Answers, p. 120**
> **1.** b
> **2.** a
> **3.** c

B (10 minutes)

1. Play the audio and have students check the correct information for each person.

2. Have students compare thier answers with a partner.

3. Go over the answers with the class.

> **Activity B Answers, p. 120**
> **1.** Matt: Exercises at least three times a week, Eats healthy food
> **2.** Kate: Sleeps at least eight hours a night, Exercises at least three times a week
> **3.** Rob: Sleeps at least eight hours a night, Doesn't work too much, Eats healthy food

▶ *Listening and Speaking Intro, page 121*

WHAT DO YOU THINK?

A (10 minutes)

1. Model the activity. Read the first statement and say the answer that is true for you. Elicit if it is a good habit.

2. Direct students to complete the activity individually. Remind them to add an idea.

3. Elicit ideas from the class.

> **Activity A Answers, p. 121**
> Answers will vary.

B (5 minutes)

1. Seat students in pairs or small groups.

2. Tell students that they should think about both Listening 1 and Listening 2 as they discuss the questions in B.

3. Call on each pair to share their ideas with the class.

> **Activity B Answers, p. 121**
> Answers will vary. Possible answers:
> I exercise three times a week, and I sleep a lot. But I eat junk food, and I never eat vegetables.

1. Draw two overlapping circles on the board. Label the left section with your name, the right section with a student's name, and the overlapping section with *both of us*.

2. Read the first sentence in Activity A. Complete it for yourself. Then ask the student to complete it. If your answers are the same, write the answer in the overlapping section (*exercise regularly*). If the answers are different, write each answer in the section under the correct name.

3. Put students in pairs to create their own Venn diagrams.

4. Walk around to give help as needed.

5. Elicit some of the ways students are the same or different from their partners.

Learning Outcome

Use the Learning Outcome to frame the purpose and relevance of Listenings 1 and 2 and the Critical Q activity. Say: *The Learning Outcome is to create, conduct, and discuss a health survey. What did you learn from Listening 2? How will it help you with the survey?*

(Students learned about good health habits.)

Building Vocabulary: Adjectives ending in -*ed* (5 minutes)

1. Have students read the information.

2. Play the audio.

3. Check comprehension: *What ending do some adjectives have? Where do these adjectives come from? What do they usually describe? What are some common adjectives that end in -ed?*

Tip for Success (1 minute)

1. Read the tip aloud.

2. Say or elicit some sentences with an -*ed* word. Elicit if the -*ed* word is a verb or an adjective. Examples: *My class bored me today. I was bored in class today. Tim is excited about his trip. The good weather excited Maria.*

Skill Note

Students may get confused between the -*ing* and -*ed* endings. This lesson focuses on adjectives ending in -*ed*, so reinforce that these adjective are usually about feelings, and they usually describe people. (Adjectives ending in -*ing* usually describe a quality and are not restricted to people.)

▶ *Listening and Speaking Intro, page 122*

A (5 minutes)

1. Read the first sentence and elicit the completion *(worried)*.

2. Have students complete the activity individually.

3. Have students compare their answers with a partner.

4. Go over the answers with the class.

> **Activity A Answers, p. 122**
> **1.** worried
> **2.** excited
> **3.** interested
> **4.** relaxed
> **5.** confused

B (10 minutes)

1. Go over the words in the box. Have students read the first conversation. Elicit the completion *(tired)*.

2. Have students complete the conversations individually.

3. Go over the answers with the class.

4. Have students practice the conversations in pairs.

> **Activity B Answers, p. 122**
> **1.** tired
> **2.** bored
> **3.** surprised
> **4.** worried, interested

 For additional practice with adjectives ending in -*ed*, have students visit *Q Online Practice*.

SPEAKING

Grammar: Modals *can* and *should*
(5–10 minutes)

1. Go over the information in the box.

2. Check comprehension by asking questions: *Where do we put the modal in the sentence? What form of the verb follows the modal? Do you put an* s *on the verb with* he, she, *or* it? *Which modal is for possibility or ability? What do we use* should *for?*

Skill Note

Point out that modals don't change their form. For example, we don't add an *-s* to the end with *he, she,* or *it,* and we don't add an *-ing.* There are past forms, but students won't learn these in this level.

A (10 minutes)

1. Direct students to complete the conversation individually.

2. Go over the answers with the class.

3. Have students practice in pairs.

> **Activity A Answers, p. 123**
> **1.** shouldn't
> **2.** should
> **3.** should
> **4.** can't
> **5.** can
> **6.** should
> **7.** should

B (5-10 minutes)

1. Go over the directions and the examples.

2. Have students write four to five sentences.

3. Call on students to share their ideas with the class.

Activity B Answers, p. 124
Answers will vary. Possible answers:
I eat junk food. I never eat vegetables. I feel a lot of stress at work because I don't like my job. I work too much.

C (5-10 minutes)

1. Go over the directions and the example.

2. Put students in pairs. Have them take turns reading their sentences and giving advice using *should* and *shouldn't.*

3. Call on students to share their ideas with the class.

Activity C Answers, p. 124
Answers will vary. Possible answers:
You shouldn't eat junk food. You should eat vegetables. You should find a new job. You shouldn't work too much.

 For additional practice with the modals *can* and *should,* have students visit *Q Online Practice.*

MULTILEVEL OPTION

Pair lower-level students together and have them discuss their stress and bad habits and give advice orally. Pair higher-level students together and have them write a paragraph about their stress and bad habits. Then have them respond to their partner's paragraph and give advice in writing.

21ST CENTURY SKILLS

Whether students are in an academic or professional setting, they will be called upon to respond to problems in polite and constructive ways. It's important that students are able to present suggestions or give advice in appropriate ways. To extend this grammar lesson, suggest students brainstorm other situations in which they might need to give advice (e.g., a classmate has a problem with a teacher or a class, a co-worker has difficulty meeting a deadline, a supervisor is frustrated with another employee's work). Encourage students to think of less personal problems (i.e., not a friend's fight with her parents). Have students work in pairs to write a description of the problem; then each pair should trade with another pair to write advice.

Pronunciation: *Can, can't, should,* and *shouldn't* (5 minutes)

🔊 CD2, Track 24

1. Have students read the information.
2. Play the audio.
3. Check comprehension by asking questions: *Do we usually stress* can *or* can't*? Is the* t *pronounced? Which word has two syllables?*

A (10 minutes)

🔊 CD2, Track 25

1. Direct students' attention to the photo. Ask: *What do you see? Is this healthy food or unhealthy food?*
2. Play the audio. Have students circle the modal they hear.
3. Have students compare their answers with a partner.
4. Go over the answers with the class.

> **Activity A Answers, p. 125**
> 2. should
> 3. can
> 4. can't
> 5. can
> 6. should
> 7. shouldn't
> 8. can't
> 9. shouldn't
> 10. can't

B (5 minutes)

1. Put students in pairs and have them take turns saying the sentences in Activity A.
2. Call on students to say the sentences to the class.

C (10 minutes)

1. Model the activity. Say a sentence with *can* or *can't* and write it on the board.
2. Have students write sentences using the modals.

> **Activity C Answers, p. 125**
> Answers will vary. Possible answers:
> 1. I can cook.
> 2. I can't ride a bike.
> 3. I can run five miles.
> 4. I should eat more fruit.
> 5. I shouldn't drink soda.
> 6. I shouldn't work too much.

▶ *Listening and Speaking Intro, page 126*

D (10 minutes)

1. Put students in pairs to take turns reading their sentences from Activity C. Their partners should circle the modal they hear.
2. Have students check their answers with their partner.
3. Call on students to read a sentence to the class. Elicit the modal.

> **Activity D Answers, p. 125**
> Answers will vary.

 For additional practice with *can, can't, should,* and *shouldn't*, have students visit *Q Online Practice*.

Q Unit Assignment: Create, conduct, and discuss a health survey

Unit Question (5 minutes)

Refer students back to the ideas they discussed at the beginning of the unit about what they do to stay healthy. Refer to their group surveys. Cue students if necessary by asking specific questions about the content of the unit: *What are some good health habits? What are some bad habits? What causes stress? What helps stress? What are some things you should do to be healthy?*

Learning Outcome

1. Tie the Unit Assignment to the unit Learning Outcome. Say: *The outcome for this unit is to create, conduct, and discuss a health survey. This Unit Assignment is going to let you show your skill in creating survey questions, asking and answering questions, and discussing the results.*
2. Explain that you are going to use a rubric similar to their Self-Assessment checklist on p. 128 to grade their Unit Assignment. You can also share a copy of the Unit Assignment Rubric (on p. 76 of this *Teacher's Handbook*) with the students.

Consider the Ideas (15 minutes)

🔊 CD2, Track 26

1. Have students read the questions.
2. Play the audio. Have students check the questions they hear.

3. Have students compare their answers with a partner.

4. Go over the answers with the class.

> **Consider the Ideas Answers, p. 126**
> Checked: 2, 3, 5

Prepare and Speak

Gather Ideas

A (5 minutes)

1. Put students in pairs to write six questions about health habits.

2. Elicit questions from the class. Make sure students are asking about diet, sleep, and work.

▶ *Listening and Speaking Intro, page 127*

Organize Ideas

B (5 minutes)

1. Have students work with their partner to choose the three best health questions and write them in the survey form.

▶ *Listening and Speaking Intro, page 128*

Skill Review: Asking for repetition
(2 minutes)

1. Go over the review information in the box.

2. Point out that students should use these questions to ask for repetition if they don't understand their classmates' answers.

Speak

C (10–15 minutes)

1. Have students read the directions and the steps.

2. Refer students to the Self-Assessment checklist. Suggest students review pp. 114 and 119 for vocabulary, pp. 123-124 for use of modals, p. 121 for adjectives ending in *-ed*, and p. 117 for frequency expressions.

3. Have students work individually to ask three classmates their questions and record the answers.

4. Have students rejoin their partners to share their survey answers.

5. Call on students to tell the class about the results.

6. Use the Unit Assignment Rubric on p. 76 of this *Teacher's Handbook* to score each student's discussion.

7. Alternatively, have students complete the Unit Assignment Rubric for their partners.

Check and Reflect

Check

A (5 minutes)

1. Direct students to read and complete the Self-Assessment checklist.

2. Ask for a show of hands for how many students gave all or mostly *yes* answers.

3. Congratulate them on their success. If students had difficulty with any of the items, help them make a plan for how to improve. For example, if students had trouble using the modals correctly, refer them to p. 123 to review. Suggest they practice the modals over the next week.

Reflect

B (5 minutes)

1. Direct students to discuss the questions with a partner.

2. Elicit ideas from the class.

3. Ask students if the unit prepared them to create, conduct, and discuss a health survey.

Track Your Success

1. Have students circle the words they have learned in this unit. Suggest that students go back through the unit to review any words they have forgotten.

2. Have students check the skills they have mastered. If students need more practice to feel confident about their proficiency in a skill, point out the page numbers and encourage them to review.

3. Read the Learning Outcome aloud. Ask students if they feel that they have met the outcome.

Unit 8   Health

Unit Assignment Rubric

Student name: _____

Date: _____

Unit Assignment: *Create, conduct, and discuss a health survey.*

20 points = Discussion element was completely successful (at least 90% of the time).
15 points = Discussion element was mostly successful (at least 70% of the time).
10 points = Discussion element was partially successful (at least 50% of the time).
  0 points = Discussion element was not successful.

Discuss a health survey	20 points	15 points	10 points	0 points
Student's information was clear.				
Student used vocabulary from this unit.				
Student used the modals *can, can't, should,* and *shouldn't* correctly.				
Student used adjectives ending with *–ed* correctly.				
Student noted frequency expressions and used them in discussion.				

Total points: _____

Comments:

Unit QUESTION
What makes a city special?

Cities

LISTENING • listening for frequency
VOCABULARY • using the dictionary: word families
GRAMMAR • past of *be;* simple past affirmative statements
PRONUNCIATION • *-ed* endings
SPEAKING • using open questions

LEARNING OUTCOME

Give a presentation about a special city using the simple present and simple past.

▶ *Listening and Speaking Intro, page 131*
Preview the Unit

Learning Outcome

1. Ask for a volunteer to read the unit skills and the unit Learning Outcome.

2. Explain: *Your goal for the unit is to give a presentation about a special city using the simple present and simple past. I will use this Learning Outcome to grade your work at the end of the unit. Focus on learning these skills: Listening, Vocabulary, Grammar, Pronunciation, Speaking. They will help you reach your goal.*

A (5 minutes)

1. Have students list three special places and activities.

2. Have students discuss their answers to the questions with a partner.

3. Call on volunteers to share their ideas with the class. Ask questions: *What is your favorite place? Why? Who has the same favorite place? What is your favorite activity? Who likes the same activity?*

Activity A Answers, p. 131
Answers will vary. Possible answers:
Special Places and Activities: the museum, the beach, the park; ride bikes in the park, swim at the beach, look at art
1. My favorite place is the beach. I like to swim in the ocean.
2. My favorite activity is swimming. I like it because it is good exercise.

MULTILEVEL OPTION

Group lower-level students and brainstorm a list of places and activities. Write the ideas on the board. Have higher-level students write sentences to answer the two questions.

B (5 minutes)

1. Focus students' attention on the photo. Have a volunteer describe the photo to the class. Read the questions aloud.

2. To help students relate the photo to their own experience, ask: *What do you like about this city? Have you ever been here? Do you want to visit it?*

Activity B Answers, p. 131
Answers will vary. Possible answers: I see buildings, sculptures, people. The buildings are unusual. This city is very interesting and colorful.

C (15 minutes)

1. Introduce the Unit Question: "What makes a city special?" Ask related information questions or questions about personal experience. Ask: *What are some special places in this city? What are some special activities?* Remind students to draw on their answers from Activities A and B.

2. Label four pieces of poster paper *(Buildings, Activities, People, Other)* and place them in the corners of the room.

3. Ask students to read and consider the Unit Question for a moment and then to stand in the corner next to the poster that best represents their answer to the question.

4. Direct the groups in each corner to talk among themselves about the reasons for their answer. Tell them to choose a secretary to record the answers on the poster paper.

5. Call on volunteers from each corner to share their opinions with the class.

6. Leave the posters up for students to refer to at the end of the unit.

> **Activity C Answers, p. 131**
> Answers will vary. Possible answers:
> The buildings. Beautiful buildings make a city special. Beautiful buildings, fun activities, and nice people make a city special.

The Q Classroom

 CD2, Track 27

1. Play *The Q Classroom*. Use the example from the audio to help students continue the conversation. Ask: *What did the students say?*

2. Refer to the posters from Activity C. Ask: *Which of the things that you listed do the students mention? How many of you like big cities? Does anyone like small towns?*

▶ *Listening and Speaking Intro, page 132*

LISTENING

LISTENING 1: Travel Talk

VOCABULARY (10 minutes)

1. Direct students to read the definitions and then complete the sentences individually.

2. Have students compare their answers with a partner.

3. Go over the answers with the class.

> **MULTILEVEL OPTION**
>
> Group lower-level students and allow them to use their dictionaries to complete the task. Have higher-level students complete the activity individually and then compare their answers with a partner. Tell the pairs to write an additional sample sentence for each expression. Have volunteers write one of their sentences on the board. Correct the sentences with the whole class, focusing on the use of the words rather than on other grammatical issues.

> **Activity A Answers, pp. 132-133**
> **1.** a
> **2.** b
> **3.** a
> **4.** a
> **5.** a
> **6.** a
> **7.** b
> **8.** b

 For additional practice with the vocabulary, have students visit *Q Online Practice*.

▶ *Listening and Speaking Intro, page 133*

PREVIEW LISTENING 1 (10 minutes)

1. Direct students' attention to the pictures. Ask: *What do you see?*

2. Have students match the descriptions with the pictures.

3. Tell students they should review their answers after listening.

> **Preview Listening 1 Answers, p. 133**
> **1.** c
> **2.** a
> **3.** b

Listening 1 Background Note

Ubud is a city in the middle of the Indonesian island of Bali. Its origins date back to the 8th century when a Buddhist priest declared the area holy, and a temple was built on the site. During the early part of the 20th century, it was under Dutch colonial control, and the arts were encouraged. It is known today for its cultural activities, including dance, art, and music.

Bruges is a beautiful city in Belgium, known not only for its chocolate, but also for its canals and its lace. It dates back a couple of thousand years to the time of the Romans.

Comprehension Check

 CD2, Track 28

A (10 minutes)

1. Play the audio and have students complete the activity individually.

2. Have students compare their answers with a partner.

3. Go over the answers with the class.

Activity A Answers, p. 133
1. a
2. nothing
3. b
4. c

▶ *Listening and Speaking Intro, page 134*
Skill Review: Listening for frequency
(2 minutes)

1. Have students read the skill review about listening for frequency.
2. Brainstorm a list of adverbs of frequency (e.g., *never, always, usually, often, sometimes*).

B (10 minutes)

◗》 CD2, Track 28

1. Direct students to read the statements.
2. Play the audio and have students complete the activity individually.
3. Have students compare their answers with a partner.
4. Go over the answers with the class.

Activity B Answers, p. 134
1. b
2. a
3. a
4. b
5. a
6. b

Q WHAT DO YOU THINK?

A (5 minutes)

1. Model the activity. Tell students about a city you know (e.g., *Seattle's culture is good. Its architecture is OK. Its weather is not very good.*)
2. Put students in pairs to choose a city.
3. Have students complete the chart individually.

Activity A Answers, p. 134
Answers will vary.

B (5 minutes)

1. Go over the example with the class.
2. Have students discuss the charts with their partners.
3. Call on students to share their ideas with the class.

Activity B Answers, p. 134
Answers will vary.

Learning Outcome

Use the Learning Outcome to frame the purpose and relevance of Listening 1. Say: The Learning Outcome is to give a presentation about a special city. What did you learn from Listening 1? How will it help you talk about a special city?

(Students learned vocabulary to talk about cities, and they learned about three special cities.)

▶ *Listening and Speaking Intro, page 135*
LISTENING 2:
Making Positive Changes

VOCABULARY (10 minutes)

1. Direct students to read the sentences and write the bold word next to the correct definition.
2. Have students compare their answers with a partner.
3. Go over the answers with the class.

MULTILEVEL OPTION

Group lower-level students and assist them with the task. Provide alternate sentences: ***Residents*** *in my apartment building have special parking spaces./If you want to **improve** your grades, study more./One of my favorite **sights** in Paris is Notre Dame Cathedral./I have an **opportunity** to study in Brazil, but I haven't decided yet.* Allow students to use a dictionary if necessary.

Have higher-level students complete the activity individually and then compare their answers with a partner. Tell the pairs to write an additional sample sentence for each word. Have volunteers write one of their sentences on the board. Correct the sentences with the whole class, focusing on the use of the word rather than on other grammatical issues.

Vocabulary Answers, p. 135
a. sights
b. improve
c. view
d. monument
e. variety
f. create
g. resident
h. opportunity

 For additional practice with the vocabulary, have students visit *Q Online Practice*.

PREVIEW LISTENING 2 (5 minutes)

1. Direct students' attention to the picture. Ask: *Who do you see? Where are they? What are they doing?*

2. Have students circle the correct words in the sentences.

3. Tell students they should review their answers after listening.

> **Preview Listening 2 Answers, p. 136**
> **1.** residents
> **2.** at city hall

Listening 2 Background Note

When city leaders take steps to make their city look better and feel safer, the process is called city beautification. Changes such as planting more trees, installing more lights, and fixing sidewalks can improve tourism. Cities often go through this process when they host some kind of world event such as the Olympics, the soccer World Cup, or even the Cricket World Cup. In 2011, Chittagong, Bangladesh built sculptures and fountains and asked their residents to paint their houses so the city would look good for the Cricket World Cup.

Comprehension Check

A (10 minutes)
CD2, Track 29

1. Play the audio and have students check the problem and solution for each place in town.

2. Have students compare their answers with a partner.

3. Go over the answers with the class.

> **Activity A Answers, p. 136**
> **1.** Parks and beaches
> **2.** nothing
> **3.** Historic buildings and monuments
> **4.** Downtown area
> **5.** Downtown area
> **6.** Parks and beaches
> **7.** nothing
> **8.** Historic buildings and monuments
> **9.** nothing
> **10.** Downtown area

B (10 minutes)
CD2, Track 29

1. Direct students to read the statements.

2. Play the audio and have students circle the correct words.

3. Have students compare their answers with a partner.

4. Go over the answers with the class.

> **Activity B Answers, p. 136**
> **1.** quiet
> **2.** a lot of tourists
> **3.** money
> **4.** the hospital
> **5.** the first mayor
> **6.** a few years ago
> **7.** hotel
> **8.** jobs

Q WHAT DO YOU THINK?

A (10 minutes)

1. Seat students in small groups to discuss the questions.

2. Call on students to share their ideas with the class.

> **Activity A Answers, p. 137**
> Answers will vary. Possible answers:
> **1.** Yes, I do. It sounds relaxing and pretty./No, I don't. I am not interested in old buildings.
> **2.** Yes, it is. The residents are friendly. They care about their city./No, it isn't. It always has money problems. The businesses that opened don't pay good salaries.

B (5 minutes)

1. Direct students' attention to the survey. Have them work individually to check five things and number them from 1 (most important) to 5 (least important).

2. Tell the students that they should think about both Listening 1 and Listening 2 as they discuss their answers with a partner.

3. Call on each pair to share their ideas with the class.

> **Activity B Answers, p. 137**
> Answers will vary.

Critical Thinking Tip (1 minute)

1. Read the tip aloud.
2. Point out that combining information allows students to use it in new and different ways.

Critical Q: Expansion Activity

Combine

1. Point out that in this book students have learned about many areas of life that can affect how good a city is: people, weather, fun, education, health, food.
2. Put students in pairs or small groups. Have them choose a city and two other units to review. Then have students use the vocabulary and ideas from all three units to list good and bad things about that city.
3. Call on students to tell the class about their ideas.

Learning Outcome

Use the Learning Outcome to frame the purpose and relevance of Listenings 1 and 2 and the Critical Q activity. Say: *The Learning Outcome is to give a presentation about a special city. What did you learn from Listening 2? How will it help you to give a presentation about a city?*

(Students learned about problems a city might have and how they can solve them.)

▶ *Listening and Speaking Intro, page 138*

Building Vocabulary: Using the dictionary: word families (5 minutes)

1. Have students read the information about using the dictionary and word families.
2. Check comprehension: *What is a word family? What can word families include? What noun is in the same word family as the verb* correct? *What is the noun form of the verb* locate?

Skill Note

Point out that most suffixes, or endings, tell you what part of speech a word is. For example, *-ion* or *-tion* added to a verb usually makes a noun. To make an adverb from most adjectives, students can add *-ly*. Suggest students make a note of common endings, or suffixes, that will help them recognize or create word families.

21ST CENTURY SKILLS

Dictionary skills are vital both in the classroom and in future professional settings. A non-native speaker studying or working in an English-speaking environment will often need to rely on a dictionary, both for written and oral communication. Students who have learned how to take full advantage of their dictionary have a vital tool for learning independence. Help students achieve this independence by emphasizing the dictionary skills they have learned throughout the course and how these skills can assist them both academically and professionally. Point out that to communicate clearly and effectively students need to use the correct form of the word.

A (10 minutes)

1. Direct students to circle the correct form of the word.
2. Have students compare their answers with a partner.
3. Go over the answers with the class.

> **Activity A Answers, pp. 138–139**
> 1. special
> 2. locate
> 3. specialize
> 4. location
> 5. special
> 6. located
> 7. specially

▶ *Listening and Speaking Intro, page 139*

B (10 minutes)

1. Direct students' attention to the photos and ask: *Who do you see in the first picture? What is his job? What do you see in the second picture?*
2. Have students write the part of speech of words a–h.
3. Go over the answers with the class.
4. Have students complete the sentences individually.
5. Have students compare their answers with a partner.
6. Go over the answers with the class.

Activity B Answers, p. 139

a. noun
b. noun
c. verb
d. noun
e. adjective
f. adverb
g. noun
h. adjective
1. architect
2. variety
3. recently
4. performance
5. various
6. architecture
7. perform
8. recent

 For additional practice with using the dictionary and word families, have students visit *Q Online Practice*.

▶ *Listening and Speaking Intro page 140*

SPEAKING

Grammar: Past of *be;* Simple past affirmative statements (10 minutes)

1. Have students read the information about the past of *be*.

2. Elicit or provide additional example sentences: *I wasn't in class yesterday. We were at the beach last week. She was tired last night.* Ask questions: *Were you at the beach last month? Was your favorite TV show on last night? What are some expressions that show past time?*

3. Check comprehension by asking questions: *What form of* be *do we use with* he, she *or* it *in the past? What form do we use with* I? *What form do we use with the other pronouns? What is the contraction of* were not?

4. Have students read the information about simple past affirmative statements.

5. Check comprehension by asking questions: *How do we form the simple past for regular verbs? Does the form change with different subjects?*

Skill Note

Unit 10 covers the simple past of irregular verbs. In this unit, students will only focus on *be* and regular verbs. Students often have trouble with regular verbs ending in *-y*. Refer students to p. 166 for spelling rules. Stress that the *y* only changes to *i* after a consonant.

▶ *Listening and Speaking Intro, page 141*

A (10–15 minutes)

1. Direct students' attention to the first item. Elicit the correct order and write it on the board *(Where were you yesterday?)*. Point out that they have to choose the correct form of *be*.

2. Have students write the questions individually.

3. Have students compare their answers with a partner.

4. Go over the answers with the class.

5. Have students take turns asking and answering the questions in pairs.

MULTILEVEL OPTION

Pair lower-level students to ask and answer the questions orally. Have higher-level students write their answers in complete sentences. Ask volunteers to write the sentences on the board.

Activity A Answers, p. 141
1. Where were you yesterday?
2. Were you on vacation last week?
3. How was your last trip?
4. Was it cold on your last vacation?
5. What was your favorite city when you were young?/ When you were young, what was your favorite city?
6. Were you in this city last year?

▶ *Listening and Speaking Intro, page 142*

B (10 minutes)

1. Direct students to complete the email individually.

2. Have students compare their answers with a partner.

3. Go over the answers with the class.

Activity B Answers, p. 142
1. traveled
2. stayed
3. visited
4. walked
5. tried
6. shopped

C (10 minutes)

1. Direct students to complete the sentences individually.

2. Elicit answers from the class.

3. Have students read their sentences to a partner.

> **Activity C Answers, p. 142**
> Answers will vary. Possible answers:
> **1.** Seoul, Korea
> **2.** a palace
> **3.** kimchi
> **4.** the food
> **5.** at a friend's house
> **6.** a big outdoor market

MULTILEVEL OPTION

Group lower-level students and provide models on the board. Put higher-level students in pairs to listen to their partner's sentences and rewrite them using *he* or *she*.

 For additional practice with the past of *be* and simple past affirmative statements, have students visit *Q Online Practice*.

▶ *Listening and Speaking Intro, page 143*

Pronunciation: *-ed* endings (5 minutes)

🔊 CD2, Track 30

1. Have students read the information.

2. Play the audio.

3. Check comprehension by asking questions: *How many different sounds does the -ed ending have? What are they?*

A (10 minutes)
🔊 CD2, Track 31

1. Play the audio. Have students circle the sound they hear.

2. Have students compare their answers with a partner.

3. Go over the answers with the class.

4. Have students practice the sentences in pairs.

> **Activity A Answers, p. 143**
> **1.** /ɪd/
> **2.** /d/
> **3.** /t/
> **4.** /ɪd/
> **5.** /t/
> **6.** /d/

B (10 minutes)

1. Model the activity. Say one or two sentences about a special city using verbs from the box.

2. Have students write sentences individually.

3. Call on students to say the sentences to the class.

> **Activity B Answers, p. 143**
> Answers will vary. Possible answers:
> **1.** I stayed in a beautiful hotel on the beach.
> **2.** I shopped in downtown markets.
> **3.** I tried Thai food for the first time.
> **4.** I relaxed on the beach.
> **5.** I walked all over the city.
> **6.** I visited some beautiful gardens.

C (10 minutes)

1. Model the activity. Say a sentence with one of the verbs. Elicit the sound of the *-ed* ending.

2. Have students work in pairs and take turns saying their sentences as their partner circles the sound.

3. Listen in on pairs as they work.

> **Activity C Answers, p. 143**
> Answers will vary.

▶ *Listening and Speaking Intro, page 144*

Speaking Skill: Using open questions
(10 minutes)

🔊 CD2, Track 32

1. Have students read the information and the example conversations.

2. Play the audio.

3. Check comprehension: *What is a closed question? What is an open question? Why do we use open questions?*

A (10 minutes)
🔊 CD2, Track 33

1. Direct students to listen and complete the questions.

2. Play the audio.

3. Have students compare their answers with a partner.

4. Go over the answers with the class.

5. Have students practice the conversation with a partner.

Activity A Answers, p. 144
1. how was
2. What was the food like?
3. How was
4. What's
5. like
6. How was

▶ *Listening and Speaking Intro, page 145*

Tip for Success (1 minute)

1. Read the tip aloud.
2. Suggest students write adverb phrases of time in their sentences in Activity C on p. 142 if they didn't do it before.

B (10–15 minutes)

1. Go over the example.
2. Have students work in pairs to take turns telling about their trip and asking open questions for more information.
3. Call on students to tell the class about their trip. Elicit questions from the class.

> **Activity B Answers, p. 145**
> Answers will vary.

 For additional practice with asking open questions, have students visit *Q Online Practice*.

Unit Assignment: Give a presentation about a special city

Unit Question (5 minutes)

Refer students back to the ideas they discussed at the beginning of the unit about what makes a city special. Refer students to the poster paper lists. Cue students if necessary by asking specific questions about the content of the unit: *Do buildings and other places make a city special? What kinds of activities make a city special? What special city did you visit in the past? Why did you like it?*

Learning Outcome

1. Tie the Unit Assignment to the unit Learning Outcome. Say: *The outcome for this unit is to give a presentation about a special city. This Unit Assignment is going to let you show your skill in giving a presentation on a special city.*

2. Explain that you are going to use a rubric similar to their Self-Assessment checklist on p. 146 to grade their Unit Assignment. You can also share a copy of the Unit Assignment Rubric (on p. 86 of this *Teacher's Handbook*) with the students.

Consider the Ideas (10 minutes)

1. Direct students to read the list on p. 146.
2. Have students read the advertisement and check what they see.
3. Have students compare their answers with a partner.
4. Go over the answers with the class.

> **Consider the Ideas Answers, p. 145**
> Answers will vary. Possible checked items: 1, 2, 4, 5, 6, 7, 10, 12

▶ *Listening and Speaking Intro, page 146*

Prepare and Speak

Gather Ideas

A (10–15 minutes)

1. Seat students in groups of four to list special cities and some reasons why each city is special.
2. Elicit ideas from the class.

Organize Ideas

B (15–20 minutes)

1. Direct students to read the steps for organizing ideas.
2. Have each group choose one city to present and write four or five reasons why it is special. Encourage them to add details to each reason.
3. Have each student choose a reason to present.
4. Remind students to review the Self-Assessment checklist on p. 146. Refer students to pp. 132 and 135 to review vocabulary and pp. 140-141 for the past tense.
5. Allow the group enough time to practice their presentation several times.

C (10 minutes)

1. Have each group present their city to the class.

2. Use the Unit Assignment Rubric on p. 86 of this *Teacher's Handbook* to score each student's participation.

3. Alternatively, have each group join another group to give their presentations. Have listeners in each group complete the Unit Assignment Rubric.

Check and Reflect

Check

A (5 minutes)

1. Direct students to read and complete the Self-Assessment checklist.

2. Ask for a show of hands for how many students gave all or mostly *yes* answers.

3. Congratulate them on their success. Discuss the steps they can take if an item on the checklist was difficult for them. For example, they can review that section of the unit and plan to practice it over the next week.

▶ *Listening and Speaking Intro, page 147*

Reflect

B (5 minutes)

1. Direct students to discuss the questions with a partner.

2. Elicit ideas from the class.

3. Ask students if the unit prepared them to give a presentation on a special city.

Track Your Success

1. Have students circle the words they have learned in this unit. Suggest that students go back through the unit to review any words they have forgotten.

2. Have students check the skills they have mastered. If students need more practice to feel confident about their proficiency in a skill, point out the page numbers and encourage them to review.

3. Read the Learning Outcome aloud. Ask students if they feel that they have met the outcome.

Unit Assignment Rubric

Student name: _____

Date: _____

Unit Assignment: *Give a presentation about a special city.*

20 points = Presentation element was completely successful (at least 90% of the time).
15 points = Presentation element was mostly successful (at least 70% of the time).
10 points = Presentation element was partially successful (at least 50% of the time).
 0 points = Presentation element was not successful.

Give a presentation about a special city	20 points	15 points	10 points	0 points
Student's information was clear.				
Student used vocabulary from this unit.				
Student used the past tense correctly.				
Student pronounced past tense verbs with *-ed* correctly.				
Students were able to ask open questions.				

Total points: _____

Comments:

Unit QUESTION

What are the most important events in someone's life?

Milestones

LISTENING • listening for sequence
VOCABULARY • phrases with *get*
GRAMMAR • simple past with regular and irregular verbs
PRONUNCIATION • numbers with *-teen* and *-ty*
SPEAKING • using open questions

LEARNING OUTCOME

Interview a classmate about the most important events in his or her life and present them to the class.

▶ *Listening and Speaking Intro, page 149*

Preview the Unit

Learning Outcome

1. Ask for a volunteer to read the unit skills and then the unit Learning Outcome.

2. Explain: *Your goal for the unit is to be able to interview a classmate about the most important events in his or her life and present them to the class. I will use this Learning Outcome to grade your work at the end of the unit. Focus on learning these skills: Listening, Vocabulary, Grammar, Pronunciation, Speaking. They will help you reach your goal.*

A (10 minutes)

1. Direct students to complete the sentences individually.

2. Put students in pairs or small groups to discuss their answers.

3. Call on volunteers to share their ideas with the class. Ask questions: *What idea did you add? What are some of your favorite hobbies? When did you start? Did you have similar answers?*

Activity A Answers, p. 149
Answers will vary.

MULTILEVEL OPTION

Pair a higher-level student with a lower-level student to help with the vocabulary and discuss their ideas.

B (5 minutes)

1. Focus students' attention on the photo. Have a volunteer describe the photo to the class. Read the questions aloud.

2. To help students relate this to their own experience, ask: *Why do you think she is wearing these clothes? When do you wear special clothes?*

Activity B Answers, p. 149
Answers will vary. Possible answers: A woman and a girl. A mother and daughter in their home. A mother and daughter are getting ready for a special event or celebration.

C (15 minutes)

1. Introduce the Unit Question: "What are the most important events in someone's life?" Ask related information questions or questions about personal experience. Ask: *What was the most important event in your life when you were a child? What was the most important event in one of your parent's lives?* Remind students to draw on their answers from Activities A and B.

2. Put students in small groups and give each group a piece of poster paper and a marker.

3. Read the Unit Question aloud. Give students a minute to silently consider their answers to the question. Tell students to pass the paper and the marker around the group. Direct each group member to write a different answer to the question. Encourage students to help one another.

4. Ask each group to choose a reporter to read the answers to the class. Point out similarities and differences among the answers. If answers from different groups are similar, make a group list that incorporates all of the answers. Post the list to refer to later in the unit.

Answers will vary. Possible answers:
A wedding. A wedding is important. A wedding, a first job, and graduation are important events in someone's life.

The Q Classroom

 CD2, Track 34

1. Play *The Q Classroom.* Use the example from the audio to help students continue the conversation. Ask: *What did the students say?*

2. To help students think more deeply, ask: *Did the students have different answers than yours? How old do you think the students are? Why do you think so?*

▶ *Listening and Speaking Intro, page 150*

LISTENING

LISTENING 1: Ania Filochowska: A Young Genius

VOCABULARY (10 minutes)

1. Direct students to read the sentences and circle the answer individually.

2. Have students compare their answers with a partner.

3. Go over the answers with the class.

MULTILEVEL OPTION

Group lower-level students and assist them with the task. Provide alternate example sentences to help them understand the words. *Albert Einstein was a* **genius**. *He was much smarter than most people./I am a very good swimmer. I* **win** *most of my races./Getting good grades is an* **achievement**./*Mark is in a music* **competition** *today. They will choose the best musicians from the group.*

Have higher-level students complete the activity individually and then compare their answers with a partner. Tell the pairs to write a paragraph or story and use as many of the vocabulary words as possible. Call on higher level students to read their ideas to the class.

Vocabulary Answers, pp. 150-151
1. b
2. a
3. b
4. a
5. a
6. a
7. b
8. b

For additional practice with the vocabulary, have students visit *Q Online Practice*.

▶ *Listening and Speaking Intro, page 151*

PREVIEW LISTENING 1 (5 minutes)

1. Direct students' attention to the picture. Ask: *Who do you see? What is she doing? What is she holding?*

2. Go over the directions and have students discuss the questions with a partner.

3. Elicit ideas from the class.

4. Tell students they should review their answers after listening.

Preview Listening 1 Answers, p. 151
Answers will vary. Possible answers:
1. Yes, I know a young painter. I don't think he's a genius. I think he's very talented.
2. They learn from their parents, and they practice a lot.

Listening 1 Background Note

Ania Filochowska first played with an orchestra when she was ten. She won prizes in more than 30 competitions in Poland and Europe by the time she was eleven. She has appeared on television and studied with other famous violinists, including Itzhak Perlman.

Juillard is a school for musicians, dancers, and actors. It is a college, but they have a pre-college program, which Ania attended.

Comprehension Check

CD2, Track 35

Tip for Success (1 minute)

1. Read the tip aloud.

2. Elicit examples of milestones (*getting married, graduating, birth of a baby, death, starting school*).

A (10 minutes)

1. Direct students to read the sentences.
2. Play the audio and have students complete the activity individually.
3. Have students compare their answers with a partner.
4. Go over the answers with the class.

> **Activity A Answers, p. 151**
> **1.** 1993
> **2.** 8 years old
> **3.** 6 years old
> **4.** 2005
> **5.** 2005

▶ *Listening and Speaking Intro, page 152*

B (10 minutes)

1. Play the audio and have students circle the answers individually.
3. Have students compare their answers with a partner. Play the audio again if necessary.
4. Go over the answers with the class.

> **Activity B Answers, p. 152**
> **1.** b
> **2.** c
> **3.** a
> **4.** d
> **5.** b

WHAT DO YOU THINK?

A (5 minutes)

1. Model the activity. Read one of the statements aloud and tell the class if you agree or disagree and why.
2. Direct students to write *A* or *D* next to each statement.

> **Activity A Answers, p. 152**
> Answers will vary.

B (10 minutes)

1. Put students in pairs to discuss their answers. Remind students to give reasons for their opinions.
2. Call on students to share their ideas with the class.

Activity B Answers, p. 152
Answers will vary. Possible answers.
1. I don't think Ania worked too hard when she was a child. Children should work hard so they can be successful.
2. I think geniuses are different from other people. They can do things that other people can't do.
3. I don't think everyone should play a musical instrument. Some people don't like music.
4. I think everyone is born with special talents. For example, some people can write, some people can cook, and some people are good at foreign languages.
5. I don't think schools should help students find their talents. School is for learning certain things.
6. I think parents should help their children find their talents. Parents know their children well, and they want them to be successful.

Learning Outcome

Use the Learning Outcome to frame the purpose and relevance of Listening 1. Say: *The Learning Outcome is to interview a classmate about the most important events in his or her life and present them to the class. What did you learn from Listening 1? How will it help you talk about important life events?*

(Students learned about the important events in one person's life.)

▶ *Listening and Speaking Intro, page 153*

Listening Skill: Listening for sequence
(5 minutes)

CD2, Track 36
1. Have students read the information in the box.
2. Play the audio.
3. Check comprehension by asking questions: *What does* sequence *mean? What are some words that show the sequence or order of events?*

A (10 minutes)
CD2, Track 37
1. Direct students' attention to the picture. Ask: *Who do you see? What do you think they are talking about?*
2. Play the audio and number the events in order.
3. Have students compare their answers with a partner.
4. Go over the answers with the class.

Activity A Answers, p. 153
a. 3
b. 5
c. 1
d. 2
e. 4
f. 6

B (10 minutes)

 CD2, Track 38

1. Play the audio and have students circle the answers individually.

2. Have students compare their answers with a partner.

3. Go over the answers with the class.

Activity B Answers, p. 153
1. in 1950
2. first
3. then
4. when I was 18
5. when I was 22
6. finally

For additional practice with listening for sequence, have students visit *Q Online Practice*.

▶ *Listening and Speaking Intro, page 154*

LISTENING 2: Naguib Mahfouz: A Successful Writer

VOCABULARY

A (10 minutes)

1. Direct students to complete the sentences individually.

2. Have students compare their answers with a partner.

3. Go over the answers with the class.

MULTILEVEL OPTION

Group lower-level students and assist them with the task. Direct them to read the sentences and identify which part of speech is called for. Then have them choose the best completion. Have higher-level students complete the sentences individually. Then direct them to work in pairs to write other words in the same word families.

Vocabulary Answers, pp. 154–155
1. promotion
2. literature
3. government
4. retire
5. attend
6. novel
7. politics
8. graduate

▶ *Listening and Speaking Intro, page 155*

B (10 minutes)

1. Direct students to answer the questions individually.

2. Have students ask and answer the questions with a partner.

3. Elicit answers from the class.

Activity B Answers
Answers will vary. Possible answers:
1. Union High School
2. 2010
3. Yes, I do.
4. *Emma* by Jane Austen
5. I can learn new computer skills.

 For additional practice with the vocabulary, have students visit *Q Online Practice*.

PREVIEW LISTENING 2 (10 minutes)

1. Direct students' attention to the picture. Ask: *Who do you see? Where do you think he is from?*

2. Have students discuss the questions with a partner.

3. Tell students they should review their answers after listening.

Preview Listening Answers, p. 155
Answers will vary. Possible answers:
1. Jane Austen. Her novels have happy endings.
2. They are prizes for achievements in science, literature, and peace.

Listening 2 Background Note

Naguib Mahfouz's early novels dealt with Egyptian history. He later turned his attention to the Egypt of his time. He explored topics related to urban life, the Islamic faith, and politics.

The Nobel Prize in Literature has been awarded 103 times between 1901 and 2010. Alfred Nobel provided money in his will as a prize to "the person who shall have produced in the field of literature the most outstanding work in an ideal direction."

▶ *Listening and Speaking Intro, page 156*

Comprehension Check

A (10 minutes)

CD2, Track 39

1. Direct students to read the sentences.
2. Play the audio and have students write *T* or *F* individually.
3. Have students compare their answers with a partner.
4. Go over the answers with the class.

> **Activity A Answers, p. 156**
> **1.** T
> **2.** T
> **3.** F; His mother took him to museums.
> **4.** T
> **5.** T
> **6.** F; He had two children.
> **7.** F; He wrote 34 novels.
> **8.** T

Tip for Success (1 minute)

1. Read the tip aloud.
2. Have students notice which questions in B ask about numbers.

B (10 minutes)

CD2, Track 39

1. Have students read the questions.
2. Play the audio again and have students circle the correct answers.
3. Have students compare their answers with a partner.
4. Go over the answers with the class.

> **Activity B Answers, p. 156**
> **1.** b
> **2.** c
> **3.** d
> **4.** d
> **5.** c
> **6.** c
> **7.** d

EXPANSION ACTIVITY: Listening Bingo (15 minutes)

CD2, Track 39

1. Direct students to draw a four by four grid on a piece of paper.
2. Write these words on the board: *attended, books, Cairo, came, culture, finally, graduated, history, interested, jobs, lived, long, museums, offices, often, reports, retired, stories, variety, worked.*
3. Tell students to choose 16 of the words and to write one in each box of the grid in any order they want.
4. Direct students to mark off a box when they hear the word. Students should raise their hand when they get four words in a row, and they call out *Bingo* when they have all 16 words marked off.
5. Play the audio.

▶ *Listening and Speaking Intro, page 157*

WHAT DO YOU THINK?

A (10 minutes)

1. Go over the example and the events on the list.
2. Direct students to complete the activity individually.
3. Have students compare their answers with a partner.
4. Elicit ideas from the class.

> **Activity A Answers, p. 157**
> Answers will vary.

B (10 minutes)

1. Seat students in pairs or small groups.
2. Tell the students that they should think about both Listening 1 and Listening 2 as they discuss the questions in B.
3. Call on each pair to share their ideas with the class.

Answers will vary. Possible answers:
1. I moved to Lima, Peru when I was five.
2. I graduated from high school.
3. I graduated from high school, and I started to attend a university. These milestones are important because I'm the first person in my family who can attend a university.

Critical Thinking Tip (1 minute)

1. Read the tip aloud.
2. Point out that choosing the most important milestones involves making judgments based on experience and knowledge.

Critical Q: Expansion Activity

Choose

1. Seat students in small groups.
2. Write these questions on the board:
   Your home is burning. What one thing do you choose to save?
   Your sister is very sick in the hospital, you are graduating, and your best friend is getting married, all on the same day. Which thing do you choose to do?
   You can take a wonderful new job in another city, or stay and help your parents with their business. Which do you choose?
3. Have students share their answers and give reasons why.
4. Elicit ideas from the class.

Learning Outcome

Use the Learning Outcome to frame the purpose and relevance of Listenings 1 and 2 and the Critical Q activity. Say: *The Learning Outcome is to interview a classmate about the most important events in his or her life and present them to the class. What did you learn from Listening 2? How will it help you to interview a classmate?*

(Students learned about important life events and discussed their most important milestones.)

Building Vocabulary: Phrases with *get*
(5 minutes)

1. Have students read the information.
2. Check comprehension by asking questions: *What does* get *often mean in phrases? What is the phrase that means* to lose a job? *What phrase means* to call or write someone? *What phrase means that you are going to get married later?*

Skill Note

There are many more expressions with *get*. Suggest that students write these expressions in their vocabulary notebook as they hear or read them.

▶ *Listening and Speaking Intro, page 158*

A (10 minutes)

1. Read the first sentence and elicit the completion *(got married)*.
2. Have students complete the activity individually.
3. Have students compare their answers with a partner.
4. Go over the answers with the class.

1. got married	**2.** got a job
3. got sick	**4.** got in trouble
5. got engaged	**6.** got laid off
7. got in touch	**8.** got hurt/got injured
9. got along	**10.** got lost

B (10 minutes)

1. Go over the example. Model the activity. Complete one of the sentences about yourself.
2. Have students complete the sentences individually.
3. Have students compare their answers with a partner.
4. Elicit answers from the class.

Answers will vary. Possible answers:
1. I got engaged when I was 25.
2. I got married when I was 26.
3. My brother got laid off last month.
4. He got hired last week.
5. My friend got a promotion in January.
6. I got injured in 2010.

 For additional practice with phrases with *get*, have students visit *Q Online Practice*.

SPEAKING

Grammar: Simple past with regular and irregular verbs (10–15 minutes)

1. Go over the information in the box.

2. Provide or elicit other sentences: *I began English classes ten years ago. We had a test yesterday. He ate dinner at 10:00 last night. They didn't go to the movies last Saturday. Did you sleep well last night? What did you do on the weekend?*

3. Check comprehension of the lesson by asking questions: *What is the simple past form of* see/give/buy/go? *Is* read *a regular or irregular verb? Which verb is regular:* begin *or* start? *What is the negative of:* She came to school yesterday? *Do you use the simple past form of the verb in questions?*

Skill Note

Point out that students must learn the past forms of irregular verbs—there is no easy way to do it. Students may have trouble using the auxiliary correctly in questions and negatives. Emphasize that *did* shows that it is a simple past tense sentence. Students should not use both *did* and the past form of the main verb.

A (10 minutes)

1. Direct students to complete the sentences individually.

2. Have students compare their answers with a partner.

3. Go over the answers with the class.

> **Activity A Answers, p. 160**
> **1.** didn't go
> **2.** ate
> **3.** had
> **4.** bought
> **5.** didn't get
> **6.** didn't graduate
> **7.** took
> **8.** retired
> **9.** didn't give
> **10.** became

B (10 minutes)

1. Direct students to write the questions individually.

2. Have students compare their answers with a partner.

3. Go over the answers with the class.

> **Activity B Answers, pp. 160-161**
> **1.** When did Rob call you?
> **2.** Why did he get a promotion?
> **3.** Where did he go for vacation?
> **4.** What did he buy his son for his birthday?

C (10 minutes)

1. Model the activity. Tell students one thing you did and didn't do yesterday.

2. Have students write sentences individually.

3. Have students read their sentences to a partner.

4. Call on students to share their ideas with the class.

> **Activity C Answers, p. 161**
> Answers will vary. Possible answers:
> **1.** I bought a cup of coffee.
> **2.** I ate lunch with a friend.
> **3.** I studied with a friend.
> **4.** I didn't play tennis.
> **5.** I didn't watch TV.
> **6.** I didn't see a movie.

 For additional practice with the simple past of regular and irregular verbs, have students visit *Q Online Practice.*

Pronunciation: Numbers with *-teen* and *-ty* (5 minutes)

CD2, Track 40

1. Have students read the information.

2. Play the audio.

3. Check comprehension by asking questions: *Which ending starts with a soft* d *sound?*

Skill Note

Point out that the syllable *-teen* receives more stress than the syllable *-ty*.

A (10 minutes)

◀)) CD2, Track 41

1. Play the audio. Have students circle the number they hear.

2. Have students compare their answers with a partner.

3. Go over the answers with the class.

> **Activity A Answers, p. 162**
> **1.** 30
> **2.** 1916
> **3.** 15
> **4.** 4:50
> **5.** 1913
> **6.** 30
> **7.** 14
> **8.** 440
> **9.** 1914
> **10.** 80

Tip for Success (1 minute)

1. Read the tip aloud.

2. Suggest students practice this in Activity B.

B (10 minutes)

1. Model the activity. Say: *I waited 13 minutes for the bus yesterday.* Elicit which number you said.

2. Have students write sentences individually.

3. Have students work in pairs to take turns saying their sentences and saying what number they hear.

4. Call on students to say the sentences to the class. Elicit the number they hear.

> **Activity B Answers**
> Answers will vary. Possible answers:
> **1.** I started to study English when I was 13.
> **2.** My neighbor is 40 years old.
> **3.** My friend John is 15.
> **4.** I bought 16 new books yesterday.
> **5.** My apartment number is 17.

 For additional practice with numbers with *-teen* and *-ty,* have students visit *Q Online Practice.*

Q Unit Assignment: Interview a classmate and give a presentation

Unit Question (5 minutes)

Refer students back to the ideas they discussed at the beginning of the unit about the most important events in someone's life. Refer to their group surveys. Cue students if necessary by asking specific questions about the content of the unit: *What are some important events in your life?*

Learning Outcome

1. Tie the Unit Assignment to the unit Learning Outcome. Say: *The outcome for this unit is to interview a classmate about the most important events in his or her life and present them to the class. This Unit Assignment is going to let you show your skill in interviewing a classmate and presenting his or her answers to the class.*

2. Explain that you are going to use a rubric similar to their Self-Assessment checklist on p. 164 to grade their Unit Assignment. You can also share a copy of the Unit Assignment Rubric (on p. 96 of this *Teacher's Handbook*) with the students.

Consider the Ideas (15 minutes)

1. Have students read the sentences and match the milestones with the correct detail.

2. Have students compare their answers with a partner.

3. Go over the answers with the class.

> **Consider the Ideas Answers, p. 163**
> **1.** d
> **2.** a
> **3.** c
> **4.** f
> **5.** b
> **6.** e

Skill Review: Using open questions
(5 minutes)

1. Go over the information in the box.

2. Point out that students should use these questions to ask for more information when they interview a classmate.

Prepare and Speak

Gather Ideas

A (10–15 minutes)

1. Have students read the steps.

2. Put students in pairs to conduct their interviews. Remind students to take notes.

Organize Ideas

B (5 minutes)

1. Have students choose four milestones.

2. Direct students to write their presentations in their notebooks. Remind students to check the Self-Assessment checklist on p. 164.

Speak

C (10–15 minutes)

1. Refer students to the Self-Assessment checklist.

2. Call on students to tell the class about their classmate's milestones.

3. Use the Unit Assignment Rubric on p. 96 of this *Teacher's Handbook* to score each student's discussion.

4. Alternatively, have students present to different partners. Have listeners complete the Unit Assignment Rubric for their partners.

Check and Reflect

Check

A (5 minutes)

1. Direct students to read and complete the Self-Assessment checklist.

2. Ask for a show of hands for how many students gave all or mostly *yes* answers.

3. Congratulate them on their success. If students had difficulty with any of the items, help them make a plan for how to improve. For example, if students had trouble using *get* expressions correctly, refer them to pp. 157–158 to review. Suggest they practice the modals over the next week.

Reflect

B (5 minutes)

1. Direct students to discuss the questions with a partner.

2. Elicit ideas from the class.

3. Ask students if the unit prepared them to interview a classmate about important events in his/her life and present them to the class.

Track Your Success

1. Have students circle the words they have learned in this unit. Suggest that students go back through the unit to review any words they have forgotten.

2. Have students check the skills they have mastered. If students need more practice to feel confident about their proficiency in a skill, point out the page numbers and encourage them to review.

3. Read the Learning Outcome aloud. Ask students if they feel that they have met the outcome.

Unit 10   Milestones

Unit Assignment Rubric

Student name: _____

Date: _____

Unit Assignment: *Interview a classmate and give a presentation.*

20 points = Presentation element was completely successful (at least 90% of the time).
15 points = Presentation element was mostly successful (at least 70% of the time).
10 points = Presentation element was partially successful (at least 50% of the time).
 0 points = Presentation element was not successful.

Interview a classmate and give a presentation	20 points	15 points	10 points	0 points
Student's information was clear.				
Student used vocabulary from this unit.				
Student used the past tense correctly.				
Student used expressions with *get* correctly.				
Student pronounced numbers correctly.				

Total points: _____

Comments:

Welcome to the Q Testing Program

1. MINIMUM SYSTEM REQUIREMENTS[1]

1024 x 768 screen resolution displaying 32-bit color

Web browser[2]:
Windows®-requires Internet Explorer® 7 or above
Mac®-requires OS X v10.4 and Safari® 2.0 or above
Linux®-requires Mozilla® 1.7 or Firefox® 1.5.0.9 or above

To open and use the customizable tests you must have an application installed that will open and edit .doc files, such as Microsoft® Word® (97 or higher).

To view and print the Print-and-go Tests, you must have an application installed that will open and print .pdf files, such as Adobe® Acrobat® Reader (6.0 or higher).

2. RUNNING THE APPLICATION

Windows®/Mac®
- Ensure that no other applications are running.
- Insert the Q: Skills for Success Testing Program CD-ROM into your CD-ROM drive.
- Double click on the file "start.htm" to start.

Linux®
- Insert the Q: Skills for Success Testing Program CD-ROM into your CD-ROM drive.
- Mount the disk on to the desktop.
- Double click on the CD-ROM icon.
- Right click on the icon for the "start.htm" file and select to "open with Mozilla".

3. TECHNICAL SUPPORT

If you experience any problems with this CD-ROM, please check that your machine matches or exceeds the minimum system requirements in point 1 above and that you are following the steps outlined in point 2 above.

If this does not help, e-mail us with your query at: elt.cdsupport.uk@oup.com
Be sure to provide the following information:

- Operating system (e.g. Windows 2000, Service Pack 4)
- Application used to access content, and version number
- Amount of RAM
- Processor speed
- Description of error or problem
- Actions before error occurred
- Number of times the error has occurred
- Is the error repeatable?

---

[1] The Q Testing Program CD-ROM also plays its audio files in a conventional CD player.

[2] Note that when browsing the CD-ROM in your Web browser, you must have pop-up windows enabled in your Web browser settings.

The Q Testing Program

The disc on the inside back cover of this book contains both ready-made and customizable versions of **Reading and Writing** and **Listening and Speaking** tests. Each of the tests consists of multiple choice, fill-in-the-blanks/sentence completion, error correction, sentence reordering/sentence construction, and matching exercises.

Creating and Using Tests

1. Select "Reading and Writing Tests" or "Listening and Speaking Tests" from the main menu.

2. Select the appropriate unit test or cumulative test (placement, midterm, or final) from the left-hand column.

3. For ready-made tests, select a Print-and-go Test, Answer Key, and Audio Script (for Listening and Speaking tests).

4. To modify tests for your students, select a Customizable Test, Answer Key, and Audio Script (for Listening and Speaking tests). Save the file to your computer and edit the test using Microsoft Word or a compatible word processor.

5. For Listening and Speaking tests, use the audio tracks provided with the tests. **Audio files for the listening and speaking tests can also be played in a standard CD player.**

Reading and Writing Tests

Each test consists of 40 questions taken from the selected unit. The Reading and Writing Tests assess reading skills, vocabulary, vocabulary skills, grammar, and writing skills.

Listening and Speaking Tests

Each test consists of 40 questions taken from the selected unit. The Listening and Speaking Tests assess listening skills, vocabulary, vocabulary skills, grammar, pronunciation, and speaking skills.

Cumulative Tests

The placement tests for both Listening and Speaking and Reading and Writing consist of 50 questions. Each placement test places students in the correct level of *Q: Introductory–5*. **A printable User Guide to help you administer the placement test is included with the placement test files on the CD-ROM.**

The midterm tests for both Listening and Speaking and Reading and Writing consist of 25 questions covering Units 1–5 of the selected Level. The midterm Reading and Listening texts are new and not used in any other tests or student books.

The final tests for both Listening and Speaking and Reading and Writing consist of 25 questions covering Units 6–10 of the selected Level. The final Reading and Listening texts are new and not used in any other tests or student books.